English
11+ Handbook

Contents

Introduction

Comprehension

Writing

Grammar and punctuation

Spelling

Cloze tests

Everyday practice

Glossary

Introduction

What is an 11+ English exam?

English is a test that often includes a comprehension (reading) paper, grammar, spelling, punctuation and sometimes a separate writing test. It is a common test for the 11+ exam. To be successful in the English exam requires fluent reading skills, a wide-ranging vocabulary, excellent spelling skills and a thorough understanding of the English language with its associated rules and patterns.

The 11+ exam is taken when a child is at the end of Year 5 or in Year 6. It is a test used by state-funded grammar schools, selected academies and many independent schools. It is used to select the children who perform the best under exam conditions, and to place them in a school environment with peers of a similar academic ability. Unlike most other exams, selective entrance tests cannot usually be retaken (although some schools do still set exams for entry at 12 or 13+), so there is often fierce competition.

There are two main exam boards involved in producing English exams: GL Assessment and CEM (Durham University). GL Assessment uses a separate paper for English, while CEM tends to mix other 11+ subjects such as maths, verbal and non-verbal reasoning with English to create a paper divided into sections. There are other exam boards and individual schools who write their own papers, and some schools will have the 11+ exam completed on a computer rather than on paper.

An 11+ English paper can be written in two formats, following either a multiple-choice or a standard layout. For a multiple-choice paper, children will need to choose their answer from a set of options and mark it on a separate answer sheet. Answers must be marked in these booklets very carefully as the answer sheets are often read and marked by a computerised system. In the standard format, children must write each answer directly onto the question paper.

As with most exams, 11+ exam papers are timed, typically lasting between 45 minutes and one hour. The introduction of a time frame can have an impact on a child's performance, so it is important for children to work through practice materials in both timed and non-timed environments.

The scope and content of an 11+ English test can often differ across UK regions, as there is a range of question types that can be included. However, a paper will generally be testing a child's ability to:

- read a piece of text or texts and answer questions on it
- scan, deduct, reason and justify
- write independently
- solve grammar and punctuation problems
- spot incorrect spellings
- read a sentence and answer questions on individual word meanings.

These skills are tested through a series of questions that include the following:

Comprehension

This is the ability to read a text or texts and understand information through the skills of scanning, deducting, inferring and justifying a response. Questions might include text types, true and false statements, ordering events and reasoning how and why an author has used literary effects.

Writing

This is the ability to understand different text types and to write appropriately for the text type asked for. Examiners look for a well-structured piece of writing that is coherent and logical, demonstrating a wide range of descriptive vocabulary, and strong skills in spelling, punctuation and grammar.

Grammar and punctuation

This is the ability to understand sentences, phrases, clauses, paragraphs, parts of speech and punctuation marks. Questions might include recognising word classes, plural and singular words, synonyms and antonyms, direct speech and reported (indirect) speech, and adding punctuation marks to a given text.

Spelling

This is the ability to understand spelling rules and exceptions. Questions might include homophones, root words, prefixes, suffixes and whether common spelling strings are correct. This is often done by reading a text and recognising where there are mistakes.

This book will help you to understand the key questions found in English exams. The Bond range of English assessment papers and the CEM English and verbal reasoning books can be used alongside this book to apply the information. The Bond series also provides a range of exam test papers in both multiple-choice and standard format.

Comprehension

"I find comprehension difficult."

So do many people. You are not alone!

"What does comprehension mean?"

The word means **understanding**.

A comprehension exercise or test can consist of: a passage or passages of text; part of a story; a poem; a piece of information or explanation; a description.

Your job is to read the text and then show that you understand it by answering questions about it. Sometimes the text and the questions can be quite challenging. It can be difficult to understand anything at first.

You need to be:

✓ a good reader   ✓ a good word-spotter
✓ a good thinker   ✓ a good detective!

① *Recognising question types*

11+ English comprehension tests may have different kinds of questions. It depends on the school setting the test or the part of the country you live in.

Multiple-choice questions

This is where several possible answers to a question are given and you have to find the best one.

- Sometimes you underline the correct answer, put a mark in a box or mark a separate answer booklet.
- The answers can all look very similar so you have to find the right part of the text by scanning (looking quickly through the text until you come to the part you need) and then do your detective work.
- Never leave out an answer in a multiple-choice test. After all, the answers are all there and you have a good chance of choosing the right one if you make a sensible guess.

Standard questions

Here, the answers are not provided. You have to search the text carefully to answer the questions.

- Often you are asked to write the answers in complete sentences.
- Scan the text to find the right part for each question.
- Be careful to provide all the details the question asks for and write each answer in your own words. Usually, you will find all the information you need in the text.
- Look at the marks given for each question. These are often put in brackets at the end of the question. They can give you a clue about how much to write.

REMEMBER!

In this book, whenever a new word about language is introduced, it is printed in **blue**. If you need to, you can check its meaning in the Glossary at the back of the book.

Exam tips

Some comprehension questions will have more marks available than others. To earn those marks, you will need to give a reason for your viewpoint or you will have to identify a range of true or false statements. Always check how many marks are available and how much evidence you need to provide.

2 *Learning how to do comprehension*

"How am I expected to remember a whole passage?"

You're not!

Comprehension is not a memory test. Even if the questions are on a different page or a different sheet, you must always use the text to help you find the answer, even if you think you can remember it.

"How do I begin?"

A useful strategy is to learn this **five-point plan** for doing comprehension.

| 1 Read the passage carefully, twice if you can. **Write nothing.** |

| 2 Read all the questions through once. **Write nothing**. |

| 3 Find answers to all the questions, using the passage to help you. **Write nothing**. |

| 4 **Write** careful answers to the questions, in full sentences unless asked not to. |

| 5 **Check** like mad! |

Of course, you may be taught other strategies or develop your own, but this five-point plan is a good way to start. It encourages you to read and think carefully before you start writing answers. This is especially important if the passage is long or difficult to understand.

REMEMBER!

Never simply copy out chunks of text! You will lose marks. Try to use your own words.

"But there are words I don't know."

Yes, there may well be!

Sometimes you may have to explain meanings of words. These words are part of a longer piece of writing, so the text around an unfamiliar word may give you clues. Perhaps the word itself contains clues. It may contain a **root word** that you recognise or a **prefix** or a **suffix** that has a meaning. (See the section on spelling, pages 65–78.)

"I don't have any idea what one part of the passage means."

Always have a go, even if you are not sure. Read that **paragraph** several times, spot the key words and ideas and try to imagine what is going on. It's better to guess and put something, rather than leave a blank.

"I can't find the answer to the question anywhere."

To answer some questions you will need to 'read between the lines' or **infer** the answer. You will have to form your own opinion from the clues in the text and scanning won't help you here. For example, to answer this kind of question you may need to:

* **predict**, or imagine, what happens, or might happen, next
* **give** your **opinion** about why a **character** does something or acts in a certain way
* **continue** the passage in your own words as a piece of writing (see the section on writing, pages 17–38).

In order to infer, predict or continue, it is very important that you are clear about:

* **who** the characters are
* **where** and **when** the passage is taking place
* **what** is happening: the **plot** or the **dilemma**
* **why** the passage is worth reading.

Who? – There can be one or more main characters and less important characters. Try to spot clues that bring the characters to life so that you can imagine them as real people.

Where? When? – This is the setting and explains the place and the time of the passage. Again, use clues to imagine what kind of place it is and the time of day or season.

What? Why? – The events are what make the storyline or plot. The plot can include main events and minor ones. The dilemma or problem is often the cause of most events. Be clear about what is going on and why.

③ *Identifying different question requirements*

You need several different skills to answer comprehension questions. Here are some examples of question requirements and the strategy needed to solve each type.

Obvious responses to the text

Spotting: These questions ask you to find information from the text that is straightforward to find. Typical questions might be: 'How many children are there?'; 'Where does the cat live?'; 'When did Monet paint the picture?'.

The skills required are:

- understanding what information is needed
- recognising key words within the question
- scanning the text to find the key words.

These question types are often found at the beginning of a comprehension exam and are usually only worth 1 mark so it is important not to spend too much time on them. This is where scanning a text quickly is an important skill. When you read a spotting question, underline the key words (names, dates, places). These words will then jump out of the text as you quickly read through it. Make sure you know exactly what information you need to find. Often, a wrong answer is chosen because the question has been misread.

If the question begins with **'Who…'** look for a **name**.

If the question begins with **'Where…'** look for a **place**.

If the question begins with **'When…'** look for a **day/date/time**.

If the question begins with **'Why…'** look for a **reason**.

If the question begins with **'How many…'** look for a **number**.

With spotting questions, find the information needed and then copy the words used in the text for your answer.

Rephrasing: These questions ask you to read the extract and then to 'put into your own words' some information. Typical questions might be: 'Describe the old man in your own words.'; 'What was the weather like? Use your own words to write about it.'

The skills required are:

- understanding the vocabulary used
- understanding how the words convey the feeling, description or atmosphere
- finding your own choice of words to convey the same meaning.

You need to find the section of the text referred to, underline the descriptive words in it, think of other words that would have the same meaning and rewrite the feeling, description or atmosphere. If there is an individual word that you don't know the meaning of, read the section to understand the effect that the author has created. You can then refer to that effect in your answer. In other words, just because you don't know the meaning of one word it does not mean you cannot provide a good answer.

Reasoned responses to the text

Deduction: These questions ask you to work out what has happened. You might think of them as 'because' questions. Typical questions might ask you: 'Why did the deer run away?' (because it was scared by the noise); 'How did the ship become damaged?' (because it scraped against some rocks); 'Why was the café empty?' (because it was a bank holiday).

The skills required are:

- understanding what information is needed
- reading the text carefully and thoughtfully
- finding reasons from the information given.

These question types can be worth more than 1 mark because the answer cannot be found through simply scanning for key words. The best strategy for answering these questions is to read carefully when you first come across the text. In the initial reading, it is a good habit to think like a detective about what you are reading and why something is happening. Look back at the text for the surrounding information as this may give you clues. Remember to check that your answer is a 'because' answer.

Inference: These questions ask you to work out what **might** or **could** have been a reason for something to happen. As with deduction, you still need to think like a detective looking for clues, but you also need to think more deeply if the answer is not obvious. Typical questions might ask you: 'Why do you think the boy cried?' (The text says that he was tired and hungry and sometimes little children cry if they are tired and hungry.) 'Why did the queen feel disheartened?' (The text says that the queen thought all the people would come to her party, but no one turned up. The queen was not expecting this so she felt disheartened.) 'Why did the cat take a short cut?' (The text says that the cat was hungry so to get home quicker, he took the short cut.)

The skills required are:

- understanding what information is needed
- reading 'between the lines' to find the meaning, if it isn't clear in the text
- thinking about how or why something might have happened using what information there is to make a good guess.

Did you notice that the responses above began with 'The text says...'? This is because you need to use information in the text to support your answer. The text becomes your proof or evidence to back up your answer. In many comprehension exams, these question types provide the maximum amount of marks because you have to find reasons for your answer. Check the number of marks available and the wording of the question to find out how much proof you need to provide. Sometimes a question will ask you to 'find five reasons'; or it will ask you to 'support your answer', and there are 5 marks available. Make sure the answer you write is enough to give you all of the marks.

Format of questions

Let's look at some typical question formats and work out whether they are asking for obvious responses or reasoned responses to the text. You can then work out if they require spotting, rephrasing, deduction or inference skills.

Question	Type of skill needed
Explain why Jai felt tired.	Deduction or inference
Tick the three false statements from this list.	Spotting
Describe in your own words the meaning of the phrase…	Rephrasing
When was Mr Sasitharan born?	Spotting
Why did the nurse burst out laughing?	Deduction or inference
Describe the house in your own words.	Rephrasing
How did the doctor feel and why?	Deduction or inference
How did Tom change from the beginning to the end of the extract?	Deduction or inference
Which statement is an opinion and which is a fact?	Spotting or deduction
Make a list of the items in the picnic basket.	Spotting

(4) *Defining words used in the text*

There are a number of question types that look specifically at vocabulary. A standard format question might ask what a word means. A multiple-choice format might ask you to underline a word that means the same as a given word. A common question is:

'What do these words mean as used in the text?'

Comprehension

11

It can be tempting to write down the meaning of the word if you know it, but this is a mistake. Many words change their meaning based on how they are used. Look at this for example:

> *The escaped lion had come so close to her. It made her shaky just thinking about it and she needed the cup of strong, sweet tea to calm her nerves.*
>
> **What does the word 'sweet' mean as used in the text?**

If you have read the text and this is one of the last questions, you might not remember where the word was, but you know the meaning of the word 'sweet'. You write down the word 'cute' and feel pleased. Of course, this is wrong because the woman didn't need a cup of strong, *cute* tea to calm her nerves. The correct answer for this word as used in the text is 'sugary'. The woman needed a cup of strong, *sugary* tea to calm her nerves. Always go back to the text and find the word so that you can give the meaning 'in context'.

Here are some other examples of vocabulary question types with a method for helping to solve them:

Example question 1

> **Read the following sentence and underline the correct answer.**
> **The football World Cup had teams participating from all over the world.**
> **What does the word 'participating' mean?**
>
> **A comparing   B combining   C contradicting   D competing**

Read the sentence and make sure you understand the meaning of it.

Football teams take part in a World Cup event and the football teams come from all over the world.

What do the replacement words mean?

comparing – checking the difference and similarity between more than one thing

combining – joining two or more things together

contradicting – being in conflict with

competing – playing against another in order to win

Try reading the given sentence again, but this time replace the word 'participating' with the other word choices to see if it makes sense:

The football World Cup had teams **comparing** from all over the world.

The football World Cup had teams **combining** from all over the world.

The football World Cup had teams **contradicting** from all over the world.

The football World Cup had teams **competing** from all over the world.

Now you can see that 'participating' means the same as 'competing' so you can underline this answer.

Example question 2

> Choose ONE word that is the best fit in this sentence from options A–D.
>
> Tam felt _____ after eating too many chocolates.
>
> A sickening   B starving   C conspired   D nauseous

Think about the context of the sentence. What sort of word would work so that the sentence makes sense?

Tam felt **full/stuffed/bloated** after eating too many chocolates.

Tam felt **sick/sickly/poorly/ill** after eating too many chocolates.

Next, look at the word options and see which one would work within the sentence.

Tam felt **sickening** after eating too many chocolates.

Sickening looks perfect, but when it is put into the sentence it does not work. 'Sickening' could be used to describe the chocolates but it does not describe how someone might feel if they ate too many.

Tam felt **conspired** after eating too many chocolates.

Conspired does not mean either full up or sickly so it does not make sense.

Tam felt **starving** after eating too many chocolates.

Starving is to do with food, but this is the opposite of being full. Tam might feel starving BEFORE he ate the chocolates but as the sentence says he has eaten 'too many' chocolates, this would not make sense.

Tam felt **nauseous** after eating too many chocolates.

Nauseous means the same as sickly, so this is the right answer.

Example question 3

Read the following paragraph and add ONE word from the list to each space so that the paragraph makes sense. Each word can be used only once.

animals   farmers   fields   harvest   machinery   sow

Tractors and farm _____ now plough the _____,
_____ the seeds and gather the _____. In times gone by,
_____ had to use _____ and people to work the fields.

Read through the words and then the paragraph to get an idea of the topic.

Some words will naturally make sense in the gaps, so write these in the spaces and cross them off the word list as you do so.

Check which type of word is needed – for example, the third word needs to be a verb as it is in a list of actions. The best fit word here would be 'sow' as in 'sow the seeds'.

If you are unsure of a word, try placing some options in a short phrase or sentence. For example, the fourth word must be a noun (… and gather the 'something or someone') so what could this noun be?

gather the **animals**   No – you might herd animals, but you don't gather them.

gather the **farmers**   Not really – you might gather the people *together*.

gather the **fields**   No – fields can't be gathered.

gather the **harvest**   Yes, this is a farming term and you do gather the harvest.

gather the **machinery**   Not really – you might gather the machinery *together*.

The best fit is 'gather the **harvest**'.

Once you have placed all of your words, read the paragraph through to make sure it makes sense and, if not, decide which words are in the wrong space.

> Tractors and farm **machinery** now plough the **fields**, **sow** the seeds and gather the **harvest**. In times gone by, **animals** had to use **farmers** and people to work the fields.

No. Can you see two words that need to swap places?

> Tractors and farm machinery now plough the ground, sow the seeds and gather the harvest. In times gone by, **farmers** had to use **animals** and people to work the fields.

Now the paragraph makes complete sense.

14

(5) *Recognising features of different text types*

Every text needs to be organised in some form of layout. In a comprehension exam you may be asked, "What type of text is this?" or "Where would you expect to find this extract?" so understanding the different text types is important. You might be asked to find some examples to support your view so you need to be aware of the common features of each type of text.

Here are some ways in which you can recognise different text types:

Newspapers and magazines

- are factual and informative
- use graphs, tables, graphics, facts, columns, subtitles, titles, quotations, figures.

Poetry

- is imaginative and descriptive
- uses words to create rhythm
- might have rhyme
- uses literary techniques such as alliteration, similes and metaphors
- uses shorter lines, not free-flowing prose
- can be divided into lines and stanzas
- chooses vocabulary for effect.

Drama scripts

- have character names on the left and dialogue on the right
- don't use inverted commas for speech
- begin a new line whenever a different character speaks
- use stage directions and props
- can be divided into acts and scenes.

Diary entries

- are personal accounts informally written
- have the day and date at the beginning of each entry
- may use short paragraphs.

Fictional prose

- tells a story through descriptive and entertaining writing
- can be divided into paragraphs, sections and chapters
- has characters or a personal narrator, and a plot
- may take the form of short stories or novels.

Accounts and reports

- are factual and informative
- are usually organised **chronologically**
- may include facts, figures, graphs and charts
- may use lists, bullet points and a summary or conclusion at the end.

Reviews

- combine facts with the author's opinion
- offer a personal perspective
- look at the **positive** and the **negative** aspects
- include recommendations and a conclusion.

Web pages

- can be factual and informative, or purely for entertainment
- use graphics, galleries, subtitles, titles, scroll bars, click-on buttons, http or www address bars.

Instructions

- are step-by-step guides which tell you how to do something
- use bullet points or numbers
- use simple sentences with an **active** verb (usually in the **imperative** form) near the front of the sentence
- are always ordered chronologically
- may use pictures or diagrams.

⑥ *Checking your answers*

> **REMEMBER!**
>
> Remember the five-point plan! (See page 7.)

Most mistakes are made in the answers to the last few questions in 11+ comprehension exercises, so check these extremely carefully! Try to remember these helpful hints when checking your answers:

> **REMEMBER!**
>
> Checking how many marks each question is worth can give you a hint about how much you need to write.

> ✓ Look out for spellings, especially if any of the words you are using were in the passage.
> ✓ Be careful to punctuate accurately.
> ✓ Make sure the meaning of each answer is clear.
> ✓ Remember that there are clues in both the passage and the questions to help you answer correctly.

Writing

Most 11+ English exams will require you to show your writing skills and your ideas in a creative way. This could be called:

- a composition
- a story
- an essay
- a description.

It is difficult to say how many titles you will be given to choose from for this part of the exam. Sometimes you will have one or two titles; sometimes there will be a whole set of different options.

You may have to:

- write a factual essay such as 'My Hobbies' or 'My Family'
- write a letter
- read a short beginning and then finish the story yourself
- answer questions on a comprehension passage and then continue writing the passage as a writing test.

You always have a certain time to produce your writing. This could be between 30 minutes and one hour. Read the instructions at the beginning carefully, so that you know how much time you have. Then, remember to keep an eye on the time as you write.

"Why do I have to write something?"

Creative writing gives you a chance to shine. You can show off your:

- wide reading
- creativeness
- knowledge of what makes writing special
- extensive vocabulary
- enjoyment of language
- fluency.

"How do I begin?"

To start with, let's think about writing stories. The other main kinds of writing will be dealt with later on in Section 12 (page 35).

(7) *Learning how to plan stories*

Getting started is often the most challenging part!

That's where noting down a short plan can be very helpful. It will help you to organise your ideas and give your writing a **structure**.

> **REMEMBER!**
>
> In this book, whenever a new word about language is introduced, it is printed in **blue**. If you need to, you can check its meaning in the Glossary at the back of the book.

First of all, think about the following tips:

> ✓ Remember that you're going to write a short story, essay or description, not a book!
> ✓ Keep your ideas simple.
> ✓ Always bear the title and instructions in mind.
> ✓ Think about who is going to tell (narrate) the story. You? Or one of the characters?

Next, using bullet points and key words, you could jot down:

- **Where?** – setting
- **When?** – time
- **Who?** – names of main characters
- **What?** – plot, dilemma or problem
- **How?** – solution

> "I don't like planning. I just want to write."

Everyone's different; some people really find it cramps their style to plan, and like to go with the flow of writing. That's fine, as long as you keep the structure or shape of your story going: **beginning**, **middle**, **end**.

For those who find it helpful to plan, the next stage of planning concerns **paragraphs**. These are the 'chunks' or 'stages' of your writing and, if you forget to use them, it is very difficult to do anything about it by the time you reach the checking stage. So, part of your planning needs to develop your story in paragraphs, using bullet points to remind yourself of key words.

For instance, given the title 'Tunnel Adventure', you could:

1 First, plan a rough outline like this:

- **Where?** – rocky seaside
- **When?** – summer holidays
- **Who?** – Ed and Joe, brothers
- **What?** – explore, find tunnel, nearly get caught in rising tide
- **How?** – swim to safety

2 Next, develop the plot in paragraphs:

- explore rock pools
- tunnel leads to possible treasure or pirates
- notice rising tide
- time is running out.

…or whatever you decide.

Your plan should help to remind you to begin a new paragraph for each new stage of your story. Of course, if there is dialogue, each time someone starts talking you also need to start a new paragraph.

⑧ *Learning how to write stories*

It's down to business! You have learned how to plan your story.
Now you need to start writing.

What are your **aims** when writing a story?

✓ **Think** about the title or the instructions – before
you begin writing, as you are writing and when
you check at the end.

✓ **Structure** your story. It needs a beginning, a
middle and an end.

✓ **Organise** your story in sentences and
paragraphs.

✓ **Entertain** your reader. There's no point writing
something so boring it sends your reader to
sleep!

✓ **Communicate** what you want to say to your
reader clearly. Your spelling, grammar and
punctuation must be accurate.

✓ **Write** legibly. Your reader needs to be able to
read what you have written.

> **REMEMBER!**
> Bear these aims in
> mind when you do any
> writing.

"But I can't think of anything to write."

Writer's block

Writer's block is a very common problem, not just for children preparing for
exams. Planning should help you get started, but if you're still stuck, try the
'w w w w w w h' trick. Each letter stands for a question word:

Where?   When?   Why?   Which?   Who?   What?   How?

It's sometimes called the 'journalist's trick', as journalists have to write on
demand to keep newspapers full of stories. You, too, are writing on demand
in an exam. You thought about some of these question words at the planning
stage, but they come in useful at any time when you get stuck. Just ask
yourself these questions; your answers should help to get you going.

The beginning

You must try to grab your reader's attention from the very start, so welcome your reader in! You could think about how to:

> ✓ set the scene
> ✓ introduce at least one character
> ✓ give some hints about a problem that the characters will face later
> ✓ use interesting language to describe the scene and characters
> ✓ plunge into the story.

Get stuck into the story and try to enjoy it! The chances are then your reader will too.

The middle

This is where the action happens, so keep up the pace. Remember, your time is limited!

> ✓ contain all the main parts of the plot
> ✓ uncover the dilemma or problem
> ✓ explore the different personalities of the characters.

REMEMBER!

You need to write in paragraphs and your plan can help remind you. If you use dialogue, each time a different character starts talking you need a new paragraph.

The middle of the story could:

You are telling the story. You are the master magician and the pen is your wand!

The end

"I just write 'The End'."

This is where you bring your story to a close. It should be quite clear to your reader that your story has come to an end, so there's no need to write 'The End'.

For the ending of your story, which may be only one paragraph, you could:

> ✓ find a solution for the dilemma or problem
> ✓ tie up loose ends – unless you want to leave your reader guessing by using a cliffhanger
> ✓ perhaps refer back to the title in some way, or explain the moral of the story, if there is one.

⑨ *Checking your writing*

All writers need to check what they have written. Professional writers pay proofreaders to do this job for them. You will have to check your work yourself, so always make sure you leave time to check your writing at the end.

It is important to keep at least five minutes of your writing time for checking. Practise reading out your writing to yourself sentence by sentence. That way you can learn to check the first three most vital parts of this checklist:

✓ sense   ✓ grammar

✓ sentences   ✓ interest

✓ spelling   ✓ vocabulary

✓ punctuation   ✓ handwriting

⑩ *Improving your writing*

You have learned and practised how to give your writing a clear structure when planning and writing a beginning, a middle and an end. You have also thought about how to check your story. It is now time to think about how to improve your story-writing in more detail.

Have a look at these four examples of children's writing. The children were shown this short picture story and asked to write an interesting and entertaining sentence for each picture. This isn't the type of exercise you will be given in an 11+ English exam, but it is very useful for recognising different kinds of story-writing.

based on 'Greedy Mouse' from *Picture Stories* by Rodney Peppé

A

one day creedy mouse was very hungry
so he went to look for some food. He found a
peice of cesees on the flor. He ate some then
he ate it all. and could not get back in
his hole.

This story has a beginning, a middle and an end. But it is very dull!
You could call it a 'bare bones' story. It has all the structure, but is not
entertaining or interesting for the reader. What could be done about
improving a story like this?

Here's a different version of the same story.

B

Greedy mouse

Greedy mouses tummy was
empty and he wanted a big
bit os mouth watering cheese.
He looked down the
advertising hall way he couldnot
go. that sar because its bone
the plumfod. Suddenly he saw a
big bit of steaming cheese.
He ate ate ate till it was
all gone. He finally went
to his hole but he was to
fat to get in.

You can see that Kai has developed the 'bare bones' writing that Lily produced by adding details, humour and more interesting vocabulary.

Here is a third version of the same story.

C

> Greedy Mouse
>
> 1 Greedy Mouse was really hungry, as the hog family never left any crumbs at dinner.
> 2 "Hey look at that enormous piece of cheese!" Greedy Mouse thought out loud.
> 3 "Mmmm, yum, yum, yum," thought greedy mouse, "that was delicious!"
> 4 "Oh no, now I can't get into my hole, but hey, at least there's that lump of cheese I haven't yet polished off!"

by Annabel

Here you can see that Annabel has added not only details, humour and interesting vocabulary, but also dialogue.

Finally, this version is developed even further.

D

> The scrawley grey mouse was as ravenous as a street child.
>
> He was scavenging for food about the castle when he came across the most mouth watering piece of cheese he had ever seen in his life.
>
> In a split second he had eaten almost all of it like a vulture feeding on a dead elephant.
>
> He was just finnishing the last bit when he let out a humungous yawn, so he squeesed his head through waddled off to bed, but he had eaten so much that he could no longer fit through his tummy mouse his hole!

by Sophie

Sophie has really developed her vocabulary, by adding **adjectives**, details and similes, using **complex** sentences and thinking about the mouse's feelings.

You can make your writing more interesting too by using some or all of these ideas:

- ✓ bring your characters to life (page 24)
- ✓ add details (page 25)
- ✓ think about feelings (page 25)
- ✓ use adjectives and **adverbs** (page 26)
- ✓ develop your vocabulary (page 27)
- ✓ vary your sentences (page 28)
- ✓ include dialogue (page 29)
- ✓ add **imagery** (page 30)
- ✓ think about the senses (page 32)
- ✓ write clearly and legibly (page 33).

Bring your characters to life

Including just a few details about your characters can help your reader to imagine them more clearly. Try making a flow chart about a character like this:

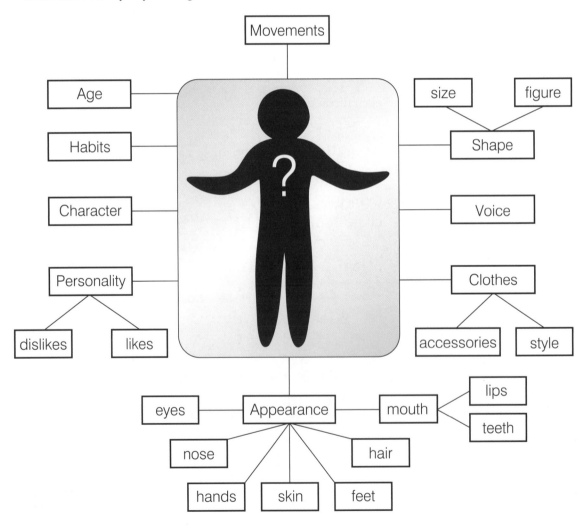

A useful exercise is to write two completely different sketches of the same character. This will help to show how different details can change the mood, personality and appearance of a character. Your reader will have a different opinion of the character, too.

For instance, compare these two descriptions:

> 1 Chris shrugged his shoulders gloomily after his defeat, his lank hair drooping over his sullen eyes. "I never seem to win," he muttered.
> 2 Chris's entire face beamed, in spite of his disappointing defeat. "It was a brilliant game, even though I lost," he laughed, his black eyes sparkling through his mop of hair.

Notice how what Chris says helps to show his personality. Also notice how the details of what Chris looks like change the way you think about him.

Add details

When you are writing, you could just write a 'bare bones' story, which has all the parts that make up a story (a beginning, a middle and an end) but is like a tree in winter or a fleshless skeleton. A 'bare bones' story is not likely to entertain or grab the attention of the reader. You would not really be using your imagination, either.

You can develop a 'bare bones' story by adding adjectives and adverbs, more complex phrases, and more interesting and informative sentences.

Think about feelings

Here are some examples of ways we can feel from time to time:

angry   delighted   jealous   excited   sorry

disappointed   sad   frightened   anxious   lonely   happy

It is easy to forget about including feelings when you are writing. Using them can help your characters to come alive. After all, different people react in different ways to things that happen.

You can collect many ideas by observing yourself and others in real life, as well as in books, films or plays.

For instance, feeling **angry** can make you:

- ✓ see red
- ✓ want to explode
- ✓ shout and scream
- ✓ hide
- ✓ jump up and down
- ✓ say things you don't mean
- ✓ cry
- ✓ stamp your feet
- ✓ slam doors.

Use adjectives and adverbs

Every sentence, even the most basic, needs a subject and a **verb**.
The subject can be:

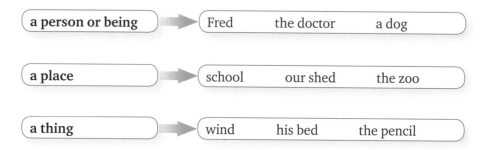

a person or being	→	Fred	the doctor	a dog
a place	→	school	our shed	the zoo
a thing	→	wind	his bed	the pencil

To make a simple sentence from these subjects you can add a verb:

Fred **jumped**.	The doctor **smiled**.	A dog **barked**.
School **starts**.	Our shed **collapsed**.	The zoo **opened**.
Wind **whistles**.	His bed **creaked**.	The pencil **snapped**.

As you can see, these sentences are so basic that they are pretty dull!

By adding adjectives or adverbs you can transform them in any way you like.

Old Fred jumped **carefully**.   The **young** doctor smiled **reassuringly**.

An **anxious** dog barked **frantically**.   His **rickety** bed creaked **alarmingly**.

And so on…

Adjectives and adverbs add detail to the subject or object you are describing.
By using them you can vary simple sentences in countless ways. So, if you
include different adjectives and adverbs in your writing, you will make a
story much more effective, vivid and attention-grabbing for the reader. (See
page 52 for more information on adjectives and adverbs.)

Develop your vocabulary

You may not realise it, but we all have hundreds and thousands of words floating around in our memories. Often, we only use a small number of them in everyday speech. The rest of our vocabulary (all the words we know) remains unused.

REMEMBER!

Your vocabulary is your word power!

When you are writing, you need to show how you can choose appropriate words to build up a clear picture of what you want to say. This can make your writing more original and individual. What you want to say, and how you say it, is likely to be very different from what someone else would write.

Be interested in words!

The world around you is packed with words, so try to 'soak up' as many as you can! Here are some ways you can learn new words:

- ✓ listen closely to other people talking
- ✓ read different sorts of books
- ✓ talk to lots of people: friends, family, teachers
- ✓ watch television programmes.

You can even learn new words while playing computer games!

A **dictionary** and a **thesaurus** are also wonderful places to find out about words. Use a thesaurus to search for alternative versions of the most common or simple words that first spring to mind. Words that have the same or similar meanings are called synonyms. (See page 57 for more detail on synonyms.) Using synonyms in your writing can help to avoid repetition. This can make a story more descriptive and more interesting for the reader.

One of the most common and overused words in English is the word 'said'. A quick look in a thesaurus shows that there are many interesting alternatives that can be used. (You may need to look up 'to say' as 'said' is the past **tense** of this verb.)

For instance:

said → uttered   replied   laughed   declared   answered   cried
stated   mentioned   shouted   announced
observed   screamed   remarked   revealed   whispered

Writing

Be brave! Try out new words in your writing but make sure you know what they mean, and how they are spelled, so that you can use them accurately.

Vary your sentences

> Ben plodded home from school. Then he went upstairs. Then he got out his Lego. Then he played with it. Then he had his meal. Then he went to bed.

We all used to write like this when we were first learning to write. All our sentences had the same shape and most began in the same way. You can see these are not very exciting sentences to read.

Understanding how to change the shape and length of sentences in different ways is an important skill that you need to show in your writing. Using a variety of sentences can help to make your writing more interesting for your reader.

You can transform sentences in all kinds of ways. You can:

✓ add adjectives or adverbs
✓ use **connectives** (or **conjunctions**) to join two or more short sentences together
✓ add phrases of time or place to the beginning or end
✓ change the order of parts of the sentence
✓ use **pronouns** like **who**, **which** or **that** to connect sentences.

See how the first sentences from the story about Ben could be transformed:

> **Nine-year-old** Ben plodded **wearily** home from school.
>
> Ben plodded home from school **and** went upstairs.
>
> or
>
> Ben plodded home from school, went upstairs, got out his Lego **and** played with it.
>
> **At half past three,** Ben plodded home from school, **past** the playing field.
>
> Ben went **upstairs** after he plodded home from school.
>
> Ben, **who** was really tired, plodded home from school, **which** seemed a long way.

Include dialogue

By including dialogue (**direct speech**) in your stories, you write down some of what your characters actually say. Using dialogue can help to:

- ✓ break up your narrative (continuous writing)
- ✓ make your writing more lively
- ✓ make your characters more realistic and uncover more about their personalities.

Look at how part of the earlier, dull story about Ben can be changed into a livelier story by including dialogue.

> Ben plodded home from school. "I'm so very tired," he muttered, "I need a rest."
> His mother greeted him as she heard him come in. "Hello, love, how was your day?"
> "Fine," Ben replied as he went upstairs. He got out his Lego and built a fantastic spaceship. "Mission control to Mr Spock. Can you hear me?" he made the astronaut say as he whizzed the spaceship through the air.
> "Ben! Tea!"
> "I'm coming." Ben ran downstairs and into the kitchen.

In order to use dialogue, you must learn how to set out and punctuate speech.

Look again at the sections of dialogue in the story about Ben. What do you notice happens each time a different character speaks?

When writing dialogue you must remember to:

- ✓ begin a new line or paragraph each time a different character starts to speak
- ✓ put inverted commas before and after the direct speech
- ✓ finish a question with a question mark
- ✓ finish a statement with a full stop
- ✓ finish an order or an expression of surprise or excitement with an exclamation mark
- ✓ use commas, where needed, to separate **what** someone is saying from **who** said it or the **storyline**.

Add imagery

A way of adding more interest and detail to your writing is to include **imagery**. Imagery creates pictures in the reader's mind by comparing one thing with something different. The two most common types of imagery are **similes** and **metaphors**.

Most people find similes easier to spot and to use than metaphors. The word 'simile' starts like the word 'similar'. Similes compare one thing with another by using the word 'like' or the phrase 'as … as'.

Similes are a very effective way of describing something in a nutshell. For example:

Her feet were **like** ice. ➤ This sentence uses something that the reader will recognise (ice) to describe the girl's feet. What comes to mind when you think of ice? Ice is very cold. So the sentence shows that the girl's feet were extremely cold, not that she had blocks of ice where her feet should be!

The giant was **as** big **as** a house. ➤ This sentence compares the giant with something that the reader is familiar with (a house). By doing this it allows the reader to 'see' or 'picture' how big the giant is, as he is described as being the same size as a house.

Many similes have been part of our language for centuries and it is important to know some of the most common ones. Here is a list of 15 of the most well-known ones:

as blind as a bat	as busy as a bee	as deaf as a doorpost
as easy as pie	as brave as a lion	as cool as a cucumber
as fit as a fiddle	as clean as a whistle	as bright as a button
as dry as a bone	as bold as brass	as quick as lightning
as tough as old boots	as white as snow	as sly as a fox

Some of the most common similes can be overused, so try to think up some new ones. A new simile can really surprise and amuse a reader. Here are some examples to get you thinking:

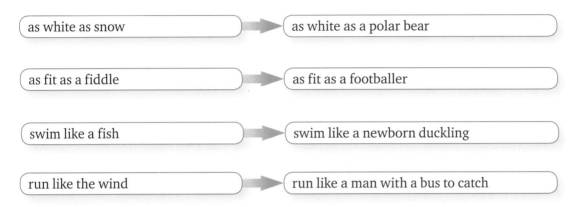

as white as snow	as white as a polar bear
as fit as a fiddle	as fit as a footballer
swim like a fish	swim like a newborn duckling
run like the wind	run like a man with a bus to catch

Metaphors suggest similarities between two things but they do not make direct comparisons in the way that similes do. They describe something as if it were something else.

For instance, here are two simple sentences:

John lost his temper.   The spider's web was covered with dew.

Look at how these sentences can be changed by using metaphors:

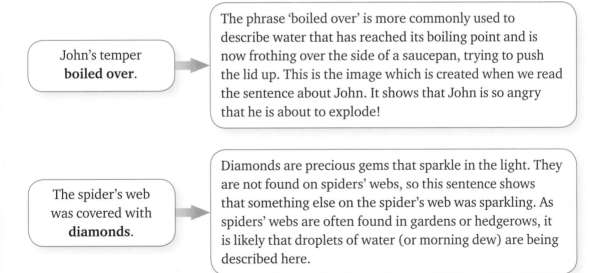

John's temper **boiled over**. → The phrase 'boiled over' is more commonly used to describe water that has reached its boiling point and is now frothing over the side of a saucepan, trying to push the lid up. This is the image which is created when we read the sentence about John. It shows that John is so angry that he is about to explode!

The spider's web was covered with **diamonds**. → Diamonds are precious gems that sparkle in the light. They are not found on spiders' webs, so this sentence shows that something else on the spider's web was sparkling. As spiders' webs are often found in gardens or hedgerows, it is likely that droplets of water (or morning dew) are being described here.

Metaphors can be more challenging to think of than similes when you are writing, but they can be used very effectively to help your reader create a picture of what you are describing. Again, spot metaphors in your reading, make collections and practice using some in your writing.

Think about the senses

We discover everything around us through our five senses. We do this by:

<blockquote>
seeing   feeling   hearing   smelling   tasting
</blockquote>

So, what have these got to do with writing?

You can help your reader to really experience what you are writing about by using words that appeal to some or all of the five senses.

Most of what people write relates to what they **see** in their mind's **eye**. This encourages the reader to use their sense of **sight**.

Adding **dialogue** or describing **sounds** can introduce the sense of **hearing**.

By including other sense words in your descriptions, you can also appeal to the reader's sense of **touch**, **taste** and **smell**.

This table gives examples of five words for each sense. See how many more sense words you can collect:

Sight	Touch	Hearing	Smell	Taste
blue	icy	clash	sickly	sour
shiny	scalding	patter	pungent	bitter
enormous	rough	boom	aromatic	spicy
glittering	smooth	soothing	fishy	delicious
cloudy	sticky	loudly	overpowering	sharp

In writing you can think of a **sixth sense**. You can feel with your sense of touch, using your fingertips, but you can also feel with your heart. (See the section *Think about feelings* on page 25.) Describing characters' feelings can appeal to the reader's sense of **emotion**.

Here are some suggestions to help you think about your senses when you write:

- Try describing a place by using all of your senses.
- Choose an object from your room and write a description of it, without revealing exactly what the object is. Try to refer to all of your senses.
  Can someone else guess what it is?

- Write about an action like peeling an apple, running in a race or playing an instrument and refer to all of your senses.
- Shut your eyes and listen for a few minutes. Note down everything you heard.
- Close your eyes and feel the different textures of the objects around you. Can you think of words to describe what they feel like?
- Think about the four seasons and find sense words for each one.
- Collect powerful onomatopoeic words which can be used to imitate sounds, such as:

tick-tock   splash   twittering   stomp   crash

Comics are good places to find these!

Write clearly and legibly

If no one can read what you have written because it is not clear, is poorly spelled, badly punctuated, or doesn't make sense, then it's not worth writing! Take trouble over your handwriting. Learn to check (or proofread) so you can correct any mistakes and improve what you write.

✓ Whenever you write something, think about these **ten ways** of improving your writing.
✓ Which of these do you use already? Which do you forget to use?
✓ Practise these ways as often as you can in your writing. Look back at the list on page 24 if you need reminding.

Exam tips

Before the exam, keep an exercise book for interesting sentences, descriptive phrases, writing ideas, dialogue that you have heard and favourite words, and jot them all down to build a collection of writing 'ingredients'. Check through your book frequently so that you can go into your exam with remembered examples of description, dialogue, phrases and favourite words. These add richness to your writing and may prove useful and time-saving.

(11) *Watching the time!*

"I'm hopeless at writing with a time limit."

You will always have a set amount of time to produce your writing in an 11+ English paper, because this is a test and to make a test fair, everyone has the same amount of time. It depends on who sets the test, but the whole exam is likely to last about one hour. You may only have half an hour to complete the writing task.

Many people, even if they enjoy writing at their own pace, find the thought of writing under timed conditions quite daunting. However, there are ways of helping yourself to use your time well.

✓ Practise your writing skills whenever you can. You will be writing at school, but you also need to practise at home. During Years 5 and 6, before you do the 11+ exam, you will need to try writing under exam conditions.

✓ Make sure you know where the clock is before you start. This is important when you are practising, and in the exam itself.

✓ Before you start, check how long you will have for your writing test.

✓ Allow about five minutes to plan your writing.

✓ When you are about half way through your writing, have a quick look at the clock. This will help you to pace yourself for the second half.

✓ Leave about five minutes to check your writing.

Don't worry if you don't finish your writing in the time limit to begin with. Put a mark next to the point you had reached when the time ran out and then complete your writing. The mark will show you how far away you were from the end when the time was up.

REMEMBER!

There will always be a time limit!

If the time does run out before you finish, think about which sections took longest to write.

• Were all those details necessary?
• Could you have moved the story on faster and saved some time?

Thinking about these questions will help you learn how to pace yourself while you write.

"How much do I need to write?"

It isn't easy to say exactly how much you should be able to write in a given time limit as:

- everyone's handwriting is different
- some people are very fluent and can write many pages in a short time
- some people prefer to plan and think first, so have less time to write
- some people get writer's block and can't think of very much to write.

A useful guide is to try and write a page and a half in an exercise book in half an hour. This is a very rough guide, though. Always remember: it is quality not quantity that is most important.

Another useful guide is to aim to write one beginning paragraph, three or four middle paragraphs and an end paragraph (the conclusion). Again, this is a very rough guide to remind you of the structure of your writing. It depends what kind of writing you are doing.

> **REMEMBER!**
>
> Everyone can improve with practice, as long as they get **feedback**.

> **REMEMBER!**
>
> 1 Plan in paragraphs before you write.
> 2 Keep your ideas simple.
> 3 Remember the title.
> 4 Use a clear structure.
> 5 Develop your vocabulary.
> 6 Use full sentences.
> 7 Communicate clearly.
> 8 Entertain your reader.
> 9 Write legibly.
> 10 Watch the time.

(12) Other kinds of writing

Essays

An essay is a piece of writing where you are discussing a title. It could be a personal topic like 'My Friends', 'Pets I Know' or 'My Hobbies'. It could be something general like 'Hunting Foxes: For and Against' or 'The Advantages and Disadvantages of School Uniform'. This kind of essay can be called **persuasive writing** because you are trying to persuade your reader to agree with one point of view.

It may be useful to think of an essay title as being like a nut, which you need to crack open in your first paragraph. You need to show you understand what that title is about and what key words like 'Friends', 'Pets', 'Hobbies', 'Hunting' and 'School Uniform' mean.

Next it may be useful to put the title in the dock, as if in a trial. That way you can think of calling up your 'witnesses' to 'give evidence' and provide your opinions for and against the title. This can help give your writing a structure. A useful way to do this is to use phrases such as 'Firstly, secondly…' or 'On the one hand… On the other hand…' to begin your paragraphs and make your points.

It is very important that you keep the title in mind all the time and not let yourself go off onto a different subject.

Towards the end imagine the judge summing up the evidence at a trial, drawing all the threads together and coming to a conclusion. This will be your final paragraph.

Letters

You may be asked to write a letter in 11+ English. This could be a formal or an informal letter. Remember, there are certain aspects that apply to all letters:

✓ write the address and the date at the top of the letter on the right-hand side

✓ write in the first person, using 'I' or 'we'

✓ write in the present tense (usually).

Formal letters

Formal letters can be written for many reasons. You may be asking for information, complaining about something or explaining something. All formal letters should follow a particular format so, whatever your reason for writing, you should:

✓ put your name, address and the date clearly at the top of the letter on the right-hand side

✓ start with 'Dear' and the person's name, or write 'Dear Sir/ Madam' if you don't know his or her name

✓ write in paragraphs:
  - in the first paragraph, explain why you are writing
  - in the middle paragraphs, add further details
  - in the final paragraph, draw the letter to a close and perhaps ask for a reply

✓ use formal words and be firm

✓ use a formal ending: 'Yours sincerely' if you know the name of the person you are writing to; 'Yours faithfully' if you don't.

Informal letters

An informal letter is one sent to family members, friends or penfriends, for example. You can choose how to set it out and how you write it. If you are asked to write an informal letter in an exam, it is still important to write clearly and pay attention to sentences, spelling and punctuation.

✓ You can start with 'Dear', but could choose other, more friendly, greetings: **'Hello'**, **'Hi'**.

✓ Follow this with the person's name.

✓ You could write in one paragraph.

✓ You could use informal words and a chatty tone.

✓ Finish with an informal ending: **'Love from…'**, **'Bye for now'**, **'Best wishes'**, **'Write soon'**.

✓ You may include a postscript (**PS**) to add something you forgot to mention in the letter.

Here are some ideas of the sorts of letters that you could be asked to write in 11+ English:

- Write to the Prime Minister explaining why children should have less homework.
- Write a letter to the town council arguing that your playing field should not be built on.
- Write a first letter to a new penfriend.
- Imagine you are on a week's adventure holiday. Write to a friend about your experiences.

> **REMEMBER!**
>
> Before you start, work out whether the letter you have to write is formal or informal.

Features of formal and informal writing

Formal writing does not have any contractions (words using an apostrophe to show missing letters, such as 'don't', 'I'm' and 'wouldn't'). It is not personal or expressive, and it is not chatty. It does have correct spellings, grammar and layout. You use formal writing when you want to be respectful to the target reader such as a teacher, the editor of a newspaper or someone in authority.

Informal writing is the opposite. It is personal and expressive, can be chatty and allows less formal grammar and layout. You use informal writing when you are leaving messages, or sending personal emails or texts to friends and family.

Here are two examples showing formal and informal writing structures:

> It is with regret that Rebecca Crane will be unable to attend the party on Saturday 3 March. She has a prior appointment that cannot be rearranged.

> Sooooo sorry but Becca can't come to the party as she's staying with her nan that weekend.

Recounts, reports and accounts

Recounts are used to 'retell' something. They can be personal, like a **report** about a school trip or a holiday, or impersonal like a newspaper article or an **account** of an historical event.

In your 11+ English paper, you could be asked to write a description of an event or an experience you have had. You could be asked to write a report of a school summer fair for the school magazine, or perhaps an account of your last holiday, a trip abroad or a class outing.

- ✓ start with an introduction, explaining what the writing is going to be about
- ✓ are written in the first or third person (I/we or he/she/they)
- ✓ have an organised structure, written in paragraphs
- ✓ use time connectives: first, then, next, after, finally
- ✓ retell the events in the order they happened (chronological order)
- ✓ include technical terms if the topic needs them
- ✓ include details to make the retelling lively
- ✓ end with a closing sentence or paragraph that comments on the event or experience.

Grammar and punctuation

When writing a recount, try to write as if you are telling the story of what happened. All recounts should be written in the past tense and they usually:

"Those are the worst."

Both these parts of 11+ English tests can fill many children with alarm. What are they about?

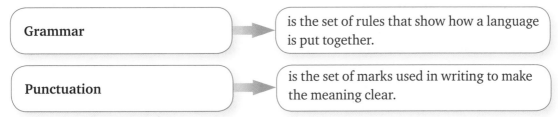

| Grammar | ➔ | is the set of rules that show how a language is put together. |

| Punctuation | ➔ | is the set of marks used in writing to make the meaning clear. |

You are already an expert on grammar. Amazingly, you learn to speak grammatically when you first start talking and then get better as you chat, watch TV, listen to stories and 'bathe' in your language.

If English is not your first language, then do plenty of 'bathing' in English! Immerse yourself in all aspects of it. Reading all sorts of different things and paying attention to what you read is the best way.

For 11+ English, you need to understand:

- sentences
- phrases and **clauses**
- paragraphs
- commas
- other common punctuation marks
- parts of speech
- subjects and objects
- **gender** and **diminutives**
- synonyms and **antonyms**
- **abbreviations** and **acronyms**
- **compound words**
- direct and **reported speech**.

Each of these elements has a section of its own here. Read through any of the topics you need to brush up on.

There is also a section on common grammar mistakes and what to do about them.

13 *Sentences*

"Whenever I take a big breath, I put a full stop."

This is quite a good way of starting to write in sentences. It will usually sound wrong if you take a large breath in the middle of a sentence. It can also be useful to check through your sentences in a piece of writing, noticing when you need

REMEMBER!

In this book, whenever a new word about language is introduced, it is printed in **blue**. If you need to, you can check its meaning in the Glossary at the back of the book.

to take a breath before carrying on. It is likely you will need to put a full stop in these places. In order to be sure, though, you need to know what a sentence is and what different kinds of sentences there are.

REMEMBER!

A sentence is a group of words that express a complete action or idea.

Here are some useful checklists about sentences:

A sentence:

- ✓ starts with a **capital letter**
- ✓ must contain a **verb** (see page 50)
- ✓ usually contains a **subject** (see page 55)
- ✓ ends with a **full stop**, **question mark** or **exclamation mark**
- ✓ is **complete**.

There are many different kinds of sentences. Here are some of the main ones:

REMEMBER!

Question marks (?) and exclamation marks (!) are special types of punctuation marks that can end sentences.

- a **statement**: He got out of bed.
- a **question**: Is he out of bed yet?
- an **order** or **command**: "Get out of bed!"
- an **exclamation**: "What a lazy person!"

You need to be aware that a sentence can be:

- ✓ **short:** two or three words, e.g. Josh wailed.
- ✓ **long:** often these are shorter sentences joined together with connectives, e.g. Josh wailed **because** he had fallen down and cut his knee.

Good writing will usually have a mixture of different sentence lengths.

You also need to recognise that a sentence can be:

- ✓ **single-clause:** made up of only one clause (see page 43), e.g. Josie played the recorder.
- ✓ **multi-clause:** made up of more than one clause or phrase (see pages 43–44), e.g. Josie played the recorder in the concert, while Anish accompanied her on the piano and the choir sang.
- ✓ **active:** someone or something is doing something, e.g. Josie played her recorder in the concert.
- ✓ **passive:** something is being done to someone or something, e.g. The recorder was played by Josie in the concert.

Notice where sentences start and stop and look out for all of these sentence types in your reading.

"I can spot sentences when I read but I forget about punctuation when I'm writing."

This happens because you are telling yourself what you want to write in your head first, and we don't put punctuation marks in our thoughts. What we say flows from sentence to sentence. The punctuation is not obvious and sentences merge into one another. You can tell when sentences stop and start from their sound, though. There are separate things you want to say, and each separate thing is a sentence. Listen to people talking and see where you think the full stops should go. By becoming aware of sentences as you read, you can also check your own writing for sentences. All it takes is practice!

REMEMBER!

If you are able to write down in sentences what you make up in your head, then the chances are that your grammar will be correct.

REMEMBER!

If your sentences have capital letters at the beginning and full stops, question marks or exclamation marks at the end, then you are already coping with the most important aspects of punctuation.

⑭ *Phrases and clauses*

"I'm not sure what the difference is between these two."

REMEMBER!

Sentences are made up of phrases and clauses.

Many people don't find it that easy to tell the difference between phrases and clauses. These checklists and examples should help to make the differences clear.

Phrases

A **phrase** is a group of words that:

✓ makes **sense**
✓ does **not** contain an active verb
✓ is **not** complete.

You need to be able to recognise phrases as being part of a sentence.

Here are some examples:

the long way home   under his coat   over the moon

Expanded phrases

You can create an **expanded phrase** by adding more detail to the **head word**. Here are some examples:

- To create a **noun phrase**, add description to the noun. Here, the noun phrase has been underlined. (The head word in the phrase is the noun 'book'.)
  The small, red dog-eared book sat all alone on the top of the bookcase.

- To create a **prepositional phrase**, add description to the **preposition**. Here, the prepositional phrase has been underlined. (The head word in the phrase is the preposition 'on'.)
  The small, red, dog-eared book sat all alone on the top of the bookcase.

- To create an **adjectival phrase**, add description to the adjective. Here, the adjectival phrase has been underlined
  The small, red, dog-eared book sat all alone on the top of the bookcase.

- To create an **adverbial phrase**, add description to the adverb. Here, the adverbial phrase has been underlined.
  The red, small, dog-eared book sat all alone on the top of the bookcase.

Q. Why is the noun phrase almost the same as the adjectival phrase?

A. If the head word is a noun (book) we underline everything describing the book. If the head word is an adjective (the words that describe the book) then we underline everything that is a describing word but not the noun (book). Underlining the noun as well would turn it into an expanded noun phrase.

Q. Why does the prepositional phrase end in a noun?

A. The head word does not necessarily have to be at the end of the phrase. In this instance, the head word is the preposition 'on' and the phrase describes where the book sat, making it a prepositional phrase.

Q. Is there such a thing as a verb phrase?

A. In English, a group of words that has an active verb as the head word is called a clause.

Clauses

A **clause** is a group of words that:

> ✓ **contains** a subject and an active verb
> ✓ is **complete**.

REMEMBER!

There are two types of clause: a **main** clause and a **subordinate** clause.

A main clause:

> ✓ makes sense **on its own** as a complete sentence.

Here are some main clauses using the phrases from page 41:

we went the long way home   he'd hidden it under his coat   she was over the moon

A subordinate clause:

> ✓ does **not** make sense on its own
> ✓ starts with a **connective**: since, when, after, as, although
> ✓ can be written **before, in the middle of** or **after** a main clause
> ✓ **adds information** to the main clause
> ✓ is separated from the main clause by a **comma** only when it begins the sentence.

If you put main and subordinate clauses together, you can make multi-clause sentences.

Here are the main clauses from above, with examples of subordinate clauses attached:

After the concert, we went the long way home.
He'd hidden it under his coat when Reuben wasn't looking.
Although she had school the next day, she was over the moon.

You need to be able to recognise main and subordinate clauses and use them in your writing.

Look at how these short sentences can be transformed by adding phrases or clauses.

> Jim was swimming. The water was freezing. He dived. His head grazed the bottom.

A   You could join them all together with **connectives** to make one long sentence:

> Jim was swimming **and** the water was freezing **so** he dived **but** his head grazed the bottom.

B You could add **phrases** to extend the shorter sentences:

Here a noun phrase has been added:

> **Lulu's eight-year-old cousin** Jim was swimming.

Here an adjectival phrase has been added:

> The **crystal-clear blue** water was freezing.

Here a prepositional phrase has been added:

> He dived **under the water**.

Here an adverbial phrase has been added:

> **All of a sudden**, his head grazed the bottom.

C You could add **clauses** to the short sentences by using **connectives** or **conjunctions**:

> Jim was swimming **while** his dad was fishing. **Although** the sun was shining, the water was freezing. He took a deep breath **and** dived. **Even though** the pool was deep, his head grazed the bottom.

Study sentences carefully as you read. Notice how phrases and clauses are used and practise using them correctly in your own writing.

In a writing exam, marks are awarded for interesting description and the ability to use words to show meaning. It's easy to think of writing a fabulous story with lots of twists and turns but in reality, you don't have a lot of time so a far simpler plot with well-described detail could gain far more marks. Although it is good to develop interesting description in your writing, don't try to put in so much that your meaning becomes lost.

⑮ *Paragraphs*

"Paragraphs are four or five lines of writing in a story."

Some teachers may encourage you to write in paragraphs following rules like this. However, if you look at paragraphs in books, you will see that they are all different lengths. There is no limit to the number of paragraphs a piece of writing can have.

Paragraphs are a form of punctuation. They show how sentences are grouped together. Using paragraphs makes your writing easier to read because they break up a piece of writing into sections or stages.

> **REMEMBER!**
>
> A paragraph is a group of sentences or 'chunk' of text that describes one stage in a piece of writing.

A new paragraph:

✓ starts on a new line
✓ is often indented (with a space between the margin and the first word) or, if the first line is not indented, a **line space** is left between paragraphs
✓ shows a change in subject or aspect: a new place, time or person
✓ is used in writing dialogue, each time a different character starts talking.

Look out for how and when paragraphs are used in your reading. Practise using them in your own writing. (See *Learning how to plan stories*, page 17.)

Exam tips

In an exam, don't forget basics such as writing in paragraphs. Always leave time at the end to check your work for punctuation, grammar and spellings. Change anything that is incorrect by putting a neat line through your mistake and the correct version above it. Wherever possible, show that you understand a wide range of punctuation marks so that the examiner can reward you for using them.

⑯ *Commas*

"When I take a breath, I put a comma."

Many children put full stops when they take a breath, too. This means it can be a tricky way of working out when to put commas or full stops.

There are many reasons for using commas in sentences.

Commas are used to:

✓ **separate clauses** in a sentence, e.g. Jim sat quietly, as he had been chosen to direct the play, and watched his friends go through it.

✓ **separate dialogue** (talking) from narrative (the storyline), e.g. "We keep forgetting our words," giggled Sandy and Alan. "Come on," Jim said, "you're not really trying."

✓ **separate items** in a short list, e.g. There were crisps, biscuit crumbs, empty wrappers and sticky glasses on the table in front of him.

✓ **separate terms of address** from the rest of the sentence, e.g. A little later he called, "Sandy, that was much better. Hey, everyone, how about practising that again?"

You can see how important commas are in making the meaning of sentences clear, by reading these sentences without commas:

> Jim sat quietly as he had been chosen to direct the play and watched his friends go through it. There were crisps biscuit crumbs empty wrappers and sticky glasses on the table in front of him.
> "We keep forgetting our words" giggled Sandy and Alan.
> "Come on" Jim said "you're not really trying."
> A little later he called "Sandy that was much better. Hey everyone how about practising that again?"

You can see that commas have much more important jobs than simply saying, "Take a breath now." Certainly, when you feel the need to take a breath, there should probably be some kind of punctuation, but not necessarily a comma.

(17) Other common punctuation marks

"I often forget to put question marks."

"I put exclamation marks all over the place."

"I don't understand how to use all the other marks."

Apart from full stops and commas, there are a number of other common punctuation marks. Here they are:

!　?　...　;　:　'　" "　-　–　( )

Some of them are found at the end of sentences; others are written inside sentences.

How many do you use already? Read the summary of any punctuation marks you're not sure how or when to use.

Finishing sentences

You know that full stops finish sentences (statements). There are three other forms of punctuation that can finish a sentence:

!　Exclamation marks help to show emphasis or emotion (such as excitement, surprise or anger). They are used to finish:

> ✓ **an order or command:** Stop! Wait! Be careful!
> ✓ **an exclamation:** What a big cake! How exciting!

? **Question marks** finish:

> ✓ **a sentence that asks a question:** Can you help? What's his name?

... An **ellipsis** allows a sentence to trail off and creates suspense, so this mark finishes:

> ✓ **any sentence that leaves the reader guessing:** It didn't take her long to notice...

Inside sentences

You have seen how commas have different roles in sentences. There are several other types of punctuation mark which each have their own job. You need to be able to recognise these marks and use them in your writing.

; **Semicolons** show longer pauses in sentences. They are used:

> ✓ **in long or complex lists that already use commas:**
> Lee went off to fetch two parasols, one red and one white; a jug of water, with ice; a set of playing cards and a volleyball, for playing games; towels for lying on; and ice creams all round.
> ✓ **to link two or more related sentences instead of full stops or conjunctions:** It was hot; the sun was beating down; we were all bathed in sweat.

: **Colons** introduce different elements such as:

> ✓ **a list:**   The recipe needed: two eggs; 250 g flour;
>   a pinch of salt; 500 ml milk.
> ✓ **an explanation:** I have two pet hates: spiders and mosquitoes.
> ✓ **a quotation:**   The note said: "Come at 2 p.m. Bring
>   your bike."

' **Apostrophes** have two very different jobs. They:

> ✓ **replace missing letters**   we would = we'd;
>   **in contractions:**   he cannot = he can't
> ✓ **show belonging**   the fur belonging to the cat = the cat's fur
>   **(possession):**   the room belonging to Sushi = Sushi's room
>   the bikes belonging to the boys = the boys' bikes

REMEMBER!

Remember: 'it's' always means either 'it is' or 'it has'. Don't add an apostrophe to 'its' to show possession, just as you would not for **his**, **her** or **our**.

REMEMBER!

Never use apostrophes to make **plurals**! (See page 69.) Look closely at where you put an apostrophe for **singular** or plural nouns.

" " **Inverted commas** are used when dialogue is written. They come:

> ✓ **before and after the words that are actually spoken:**
> "Come here," called Akshay, "and I'll tell you the secret."

- **Hyphens** have two main jobs. They:

> ✓ **join two or more words together to make a new idea:**
> father-in-law   part-time   self-confidence   sixty-three   non-stick
> ✓ **split a word at the end of a** syllable **if the whole word will not fit on one line:**
> It was getting late and Ella noticed that the air around her was grow-
> ing cooler.

– **Dashes** can be used alone or in pairs.

A single dash:

> ✓ **attaches an extra point to a sentence:**
> He thought it was his cat under the bed – but was it?

REMEMBER!

Dashes are often used in informal writing and in dialogue.

A pair of dashes:

✓ **separates non-essential information from the rest of a sentence:**
Our first house – the one in the town centre – had a small garden.

( ) Brackets always come in pairs. They are used to:

✓ **insert useful (but not essential) details in a sentence, like dashes:**
Our first house (the one in the town centre) had a small garden.
✓ **separate numbers and abbreviations from the rest of a sentence:**
His flight (no. LHR 7604) went from London Heathrow airport (LHR).

Look out for all kinds of punctuation in your reading and ask yourself, whenever you see a punctuation mark, what it is for. Practise using the punctuation you see in your own writing. Especially look out for how speech is punctuated and the use of inverted commas, commas and paragraphs.

> **REMEMBER!**
> Where pairs of dashes or brackets are used to add extra information, we call this parenthesis.

18 *Parts of speech*

Words are divided into different groups depending on their use. In 11+ English you must show that you know the main groups. These are:

* nouns
* prepositions
* connectives (or conjunctions).
* pronouns
* adjectives
* verbs
* adverbs

First, you need to learn the different job each group does in English grammar. A brief summary of each of these word groups is given in this section. Read through any that you need to brush up on.

Nouns

* **Common nouns** are **general names** of people, places, feelings, things and events. For example:

people:	crowd	teacher	police officer
places:	school	garden	supermarket
feelings:	fear	happiness	curiosity
things:	balloon	air	computer
events:	party	holiday	sports day

- Proper nouns are **special names** (or titles) of people, places, things or events. For example:

people:	Tom	Mum	Mr Scott
places:	Birmingham	Spain	Derbyshire
things:	July	Lego	Rolls Royce
events:	Christmas	Yom Kippur	Diwali

- Abstract nouns are names of **concepts** or **ideas**. For example:

  beauty   love   appearance   vacancy   leadership

- Collective nouns are names of **groups** or **collections** of things. For example:

  flock of sheep   board of directors   swarm of bees   bunch of flowers

Verbs

- Verbs can be:

doing words:	jump	swim	read
being words:	like	know	am

- Verbs must agree with the singular or plural subject of a sentence. (See Section 19.)

  I am hungry.   **You are** hungry.   **He is** hungry.   **They are** hungry.

- The **tense** of a verb tells you **when** something is happening:

  present: **I go** to the shops.   Or   **I am going** to the shops.
  past: **I went** to the shops and **I bought** some bread.

- For both the present and the past, there are four main tenses. Here are examples of each:

Present simple
I go. They think.
He eats. We jump.

Past simple
I went. They thought.
He ate. We jumped.

Present progressive (continuous)
I am going. They are thinking.
He is eating. We are jumping.

Past progressive (continuous)
I was going. They were thinking.
He was eating. We were jumping.

Present perfect
I have gone. They have thought.
He has eaten. We have jumped.

Past perfect
I had gone. They had thought.
He had eaten. We had jumped.

Present perfect progressive (continuous)
I have been going. They have been thinking.
He has been eating. We have been jumping.

Past perfect progressive (continuous)
I had been going. They had been thinking.
He had been eating. We had been jumping.

- Some of these tenses are formed using the **auxiliary verbs 'to have'** and **'to be'**. They are sometimes called 'helpers' and are used with other verbs in sentences:

I **am** going home.   We **have** lost our cat.   Our neighbours **are** looking for it.

- **Modal verbs** are also verbs that help other verbs. They include:

must   may   might   can   could   will   would   shall   should

and their negatives:

mustn't   shouldn't   couldn't, etc.

Modal verbs are a fantastic way to indicate the **possibility** (or not) of something happening. Look at these examples of how the modal verb subtly changes these sentences:

I **might** go out.   ("Then again, I might not – I am undecided.")

I **could** go out.   (It's an option.)

I **would** go out.   ("I would go out, but… I have an excuse!")

I **should** go out.   ("I don't really want to go out, but I feel it is my duty to do so.")

- Modal verbs can help to make verbs that refer to the future.

I **will** go out.   I **shall** go out.

We can also talk about future events using 'going to':

I **am going to** go out.

People used to talk about a 'future tense' but in fact there isn't one! Instead all these are examples of the present tense being used to show that something will happen in the future.

- The **subjunctive form** of a verb is used when we express things that should or could happen. We can spot the subjunctive form if the form 'to be' is different when we are referring to ourselves, e.g. 'I was' becomes 'I were'. We can also spot it if the final 's' at the end of the verb is removed, e.g. 'I suggest she sings to me' becomes 'I suggest she sing to me'.

> **REMEMBER!**
>
> Verbs are action words. They tell you what is happening to the subject or noun in a sentence.
>
> The base form of a verb is called the **infinitive**. It usually has 'to' in front:
>
> to do   to jump
> to swim   to read
> to like   to know
> to be

Look at the following examples. The sentences on the left have been rewritten on the right to include the subjunctive form of the verb:

I wish I **was** able to suggest it.

I wish I **were** able to suggest it.

If I **was** in charge for the day...

If I **were** in charge for the day...

I suggest he **writes** to her.

I suggest he **write** to her.

I insist they **are** removed.

I insist they **be** removed.

Adjectives

- Adjectives can **describe**:

> **REMEMBER!**
> Adjectives describe nouns and pronouns.

colour:	golden	green	transparent
size:	enormous	medium	tiny
mood:	happy	miserable	uncertain

- Adjectives can also **compare** things. There are three groups of comparing adjectives:

simple:	A hedgehog is small.	(No ending is added to the adjective.)
comparative:	A mouse is smaller.	('-er' is added to the adjective.)
superlative:	An ant is the smallest.	('-est' is added to the adjective.)

These endings are usually added to adjectives with **one syllable** or adjectives with **two syllables that end in '-y'**. The words '**more**' or '**most**' are written before adjectives with two or more syllables instead of these endings, e.g.

This book is **more** helpful.   This is the **most** popular book.

Adverbs

- Adverbs describe **how, when, where** and **how often** something happens:

> **REMEMBER!**
> Adverbs usually describe verbs.

how:	He ran **slowly**.	She read **quietly**.
when:	They arrived **early**.	The shop opened **late**.
where:	The boys played football **outside**.	She walked **upstairs**.
how often:	I practised my trumpet **regularly**.	You **often** go to visit her.

- **Fronted adverbials** are adverbs or adverbial phrases that are placed at the front of the sentence for effect. A fronted adverbial is always followed by a comma. Look at these sentences with the adverbial moved to the front of the sentence:

The boys played football outside in the snow.   **Outside in the snow**, the boys played football.

I practised my trumpet every evening.   **Every evening**, I practised my trumpet.

- **Time adverbials** are used to structure order in texts. The time adverbials include first, next, then, finally, now, often, later, daily, monthly and yearly. Here are some examples of time adverbials used in sentences:

I can meet you **later**.   We are on our way **now**.   Who is coming **next**?

Time adverbials may not always be at the end or in the middle of a sentence. They can also be placed at the beginning, to make a fronted adverbial.

Tomorrow, we are going out.   **Finally**, I can rest in peace!   **Then**, we just walked.

Pronouns

There are two groups of pronouns that replace common and proper nouns in particular ways: personal and possessive pronouns.

> **REMEMBER!**
>
> Pronouns can be used instead of nouns.

- **Personal** pronouns can be singular or plural:

Jackie left for school at 7.30 a.m.   = **She** left for school at 7.30 a.m.

Paul and Amruta worked on **the project** together.   = **They** worked on **it** together.

Ted and I went to see **Matthew and Evie**.   = **We** went to see **them**.

Has **Danny** seen **the film**?   = Has **he** seen **it**?

- **Possessive** pronouns tell us who or what owns or has something:

That bike belongs to **Kang**.   = That bike is **his**.
                                       OR It's **his**.

This book belongs to **me**.   = This book is **mine**.

The new car belongs to **Jo and Kim**.   = The new car is **theirs**.
                                               OR It's **theirs**.

The house belongs to **us**.   = The house is **ours**.

There are two other kinds of pronouns that are often used in sentences:

- **Relative pronouns** introduce information about a noun or a pronoun. They include the words **which**, **where**, **when**, **who**, **whose** and **that**. A clause that begins with a relative pronoun is called a **relative clause**.

  Here are some examples:

  I don't like the cat **which** catches the baby birds.

  Here is the village **where** Kirsty lives.

  He doesn't like the summer **when** it is too hot.

  There's the man **who** works at the shop.

  She is the woman **whose** car was damaged.

  I wrote a card **that** I posted yesterday.

- **Indefinite pronouns** refer generally to people or things:

Tell me all that you know.	= Tell me **everything**.
Tell me a thing you know.	= Tell me **something**.
Tell me one thing or other you know.	= Tell me **anything**. OR Tell me **nothing**.
Show me all the people there.	= Show me **everyone**.
Show me one person there.	= Show me **someone**.
Show me one person or another there.	= Show me **anyone**. OR Show me **no one**.

Prepositions

Prepositions **link** nouns and pronouns to other parts of a sentence. They show:

> **REMEMBER!**
>
> 'Pre-' means 'before' or 'in front of'. A preposition is written in front of a noun.

- **position:**   **in** the room   **behind** the house   **near** the school
- **direction:**   **up** the stairs   **through** the window   **over** the fence
- **time:**   **during** break   **before** assembly   **on** Saturday

Connectives (or conjunctions)

Connectives can be:

- **short words:**   if   but   then   so   while
- **compound words:**
  however   meanwhile   therefore   nevertheless   whereas
- **short phrases:** because of   as a result   due to   on the other hand

> **REMEMBER!**
>
> Connectives **connect** (or join) clauses or sentences together to make more complex sentences.

(See page 60 for more details on compound words.)

Determiners

A **determiner** is a word that goes before a noun. There are several types of determiners. Here are the types of determiners with some examples:

Articles	Demonstratives	Numbers	Ordinals	Possessives	Quantifiers
a	that	fifty-two	first	her	all
an	these	four	last	his	every
the	this	one hundred	next	my	more
	those	six	sixtieth	their	none
		twenty	third	your	some

- We use '**a**' before any word that begins with a consonant.
  For example: a ball, a taxi, a girl.
- We use '**an**' before any word that begins with a vowel.
  For example: an action, an elephant, an owl.
- We use '**an**' before any word that sounds as though it begins
  with a vowel even if the letter is actually a consonant.
  For example, an hour, an honour, an heir.

Once you understand these main parts of speech, you need to be able to spot them in your reading and use them in your writing.

(19) *Subjects and objects*

"These words sound the same to me!"

Yes, many people find them a little confusing. Working through this section should help to make them clearer.

Most complete statements and questions have a subject and a verb. Orders and exclamations often leave out one or both of these.

The **subject** of a sentence is usually a common or proper noun or a noun phrase (a group of words including a noun). Remember:

> ✓ a noun can be replaced by a pronoun
> ✓ a subject can be singular or plural
> ✓ a verb must agree with its subject.

REMEMBER!

The subject of a clause or sentence is **what** or **who** it is about.

Look at these examples:

Chang looked in the shed.

> Chang is doing the action in this sentence, so '**Chang**', a singular proper noun, is the subject.

The bikes were gone.

> '**The bikes**', a plural common noun, are the subject in this sentence and the verb agrees with them.

Poor Chang looked in the shed.

> In this sentence, the noun phrase, '**Poor Chang**', is the subject.

He wanted to fetch the mountain bikes. They were gone.

> The subjects are pronouns: '**He**' and '**They**'.

Often, a sentence has an **object**. An object is affected in some way by the **action** of the subject and the verb.

Look again at this sentence:

Chang looked in the shed.

> '**Chang**' is the subject.

> '**looked**' is the verb.

> '**the shed**' is the object affected by the subject and the verb.

Look at this sentence:

He wanted to fetch the bikes.

> '**He**' is the subject.

> '**wanted to fetch**' is the verb.

> '**the bikes**' is the object.

(20) *Gender and diminutives*

"I find these words quite hard to remember."

They can look rather off-putting. But they will come in very useful once you understand them.

In 11+ English you may need to show that you know the **gender** of nouns: whether they are masculine or feminine.

Many nouns have different words for male and female types. Sometimes the suffix '–ess' is added to a male word to make the female version. Look at these examples.

Masculine	Feminine	Masculine	Feminine
hero	heroine	father	mother
prince	princess	count	countess
lord	lady	gander	goose
nephew	niece	fox	vixen

You also need to know the **diminutive** forms of some nouns for 11+ English. In the case of animals, diminutives mean their babies or young. In the case of objects, diminutives mean **smaller versions** of them.

> **REMEMBER!**
>
> **Diminutive** means a smaller version of something.

Some diminutives are formed by adding a **prefix** or a **suffix** to a root word. (See pages 75–78.) Look at the examples below.

Larger form	Diminutive form	Larger form	Diminutive form
bus	minibus	goose	gosling
book	booklet	pig	piglet
kitchen	kitchenette	organism	microorganism

Diminutives can be used as **nicknames** for first names. For instance, Nicholas is often shortened to Nick. Here are some more examples:

Full first name	Diminutive form	Full first name	Diminutive form
Christina	Chris	Matthew	Matt
Victor	Vic	Rajesh	Raj
Elisabeth	Liz	Rebecca	Becky

(21) *Synonyms and antonyms*

"I get a bit muddled with these."

You may need to show that you know what these words mean in 11+ English.

Using synonyms in your writing helps to avoid repetition and can make your writing more interesting. (See page 27.)

Synonyms are words which have the same or similar meanings. For instance, here are some synonyms for the word 'large':

grand   big   sizeable   huge   bulky

significant   substantial

> **REMEMBER!**
>
> Synonyms are **similar**. Antonyms are **opposite**.

> **REMEMBER!**
>
> A thesaurus is a good source of synonyms and antonyms.

Antonyms are words which have opposite meanings. For instance, here are some antonyms for the word 'large':

little   small   minute   tiny   skinny

insignificant   miniature

Not all words have opposites – there are no antonyms for the word 'green' for example.

Always think about meanings before using synonyms and antonyms. In English, we have many words with dozens of different meanings. If you look up words like 'mark' or 'catch' or 'play' in a dictionary, you will find numbers showing several versions of the same word and explaining the different meanings.

The words you choose must always fit the **context** (meaning) of a sentence. You may also need to think about parts of speech. (See page 49.)

Look at these examples:

The parcel felt very **light**.

The colour of my walls is **light** blue.

There are many synonyms for the word 'light'. For example:

glow; weightless; insubstantial; ignite; delicate; soft; pale; elegant; bright.

All of these have different meanings and you need to understand the context of the sentence before choosing a synonym. In this example, 'light' means 'not heavy', so **'insubstantial'** would be a good synonym to use here.

There are also many antonyms for the word 'light'. For example:

dark; gloomy; shade; heavy; serious; sinister; extinguish.

You can't choose the most appropriate antonym if you haven't understood the meaning of 'light' in the sentence. In this sentence, 'light' means 'pale', so **'dark'** would be a suitable antonym.

I switched on the **light**.

In this example, the word 'light' is a **noun**, not an **adjective**. This means suitable synonyms would be **'lamp'**, **'torch'** or **'lantern'**. For this meaning, 'light' has no antonym.

(22) *Abbreviations and acronyms*

"There are hundreds!"

Yes, there are, but no one expects you to know them all! Many individual words and groups of words are often shortened when used in speech or writing. You should make sure you are familiar with some of the most common abbreviations and that you can recognise some useful acronyms.

Here are some common abbreviations, which use part of the original word:

Abbreviation	Full word
bike	bicycle
fridge	refrigerator
photo	photograph
phone	telephone
rhino	rhinoceros

Did you know that all of the words in the left-hand column were abbreviations?

Abbreviations can also be formed from the first letters (initials) of the words being shortened. For example:

Abbreviation	Full phrase
BBC	British Broadcasting Corporation
CD	compact disc
HGV	heavy goods vehicle
PC	personal computer or Police Constable
RSPB	Royal Society for the Protection of Birds

REMEMBER!

Abbreviations are shortened versions of words.

Some other commonly used abbreviations come from **Latin**. For these you will need to understand what the phrase means rather than learn the Latin words they stand for. The examples below are often used in writing:

Abbreviation	Full meaning
a.m.	before noon
e.g.	for example
etc.	and so on
PS	written afterwards
v.	against

REMEMBER!

Note how each letter is pronounced in these abbreviations.

An acronym is a form of abbreviation which is usually made up of the initial letters of the group of words being shortened. Acronyms are different to the abbreviations listed in the second table on page 59, as they are pronounced as single words.

Here are some acronyms you may recognise:

Acronym	Full phrase
FIFA	**F**édération **I**nternationale de **F**ootball **A**ssociation
Laser	**l**ight **a**mplification by **s**timulated **e**mission of **r**adiation
NATO	**N**orth **A**tlantic **T**reaty **O**rganisation
Ofsted	**O**ffice **f**or **St**andards in **Ed**ucation
RAM	**r**andom-**a**ccess **m**emory

(23) *Compound words*

"I'm not quite sure what they are."

Many people find compound words puzzling.

Compound words are made by joining two or three smaller words together to make a longer one.

Here are two examples of compound words:

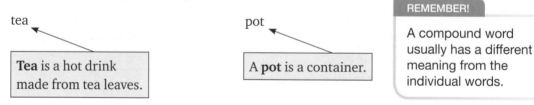

REMEMBER!
A compound word usually has a different meaning from the individual words.

Put together, the two words make a new idea: **teapot** (a covered pot with a spout in which tea is brewed).

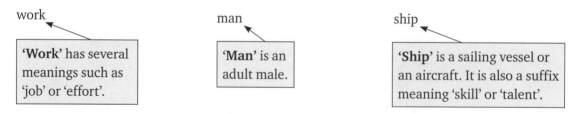

Put together, the three words make a new idea:
workmanship (the talent of a skilled manual worker).

(24) *Direct and reported speech*

"I find changing from one to the other tricky."

It can be quite tricky; there is a lot to think about.

There are two ways of writing speech which you need to be familiar with.

- Direct speech uses the words that are actually spoken, for instance:
  Jarek called, **"Help me! I'm drowning!"**

- Reported speech explains what was said but does not use the exact words. You can write the same thing as if you are reporting something.
  So, in reported speech, the above example could be written as:

Jarek called for help because he thought he was drowning.

Notice especially how the **tense** changes between direct and reported speech. In the first example, Jarek's words are written in the **present** tense. When his words are written as reported speech, the sentence is written in the **past** tense. This is quite tricky and you need to practise changing one to the other. Look out for both kinds of speech in your reading.

(25) *Avoiding common errors: what NOT to do!*

There are some common grammar traps that people often fall into. If you know about them, you can try to avoid them. Here are some of the main ones:

Double negatives

If you use two negative words in a phrase or sentence, this is called a **double negative**. Here are some examples:

We **don't** have **no** money.

There **weren't no** sweets left in the jar.

If you really think about them, the two negatives cancel each other out, so the sentences actually mean:

We **do** have money.

There **were** sweets left in the jar.

To avoid this problem you have to use the words '**any**' or '**no**'. For instance, the first example of double negatives could be correctly written as:

We don't have **any** money.   OR   We have **no** money.

How should the second example be written?

When you are writing dialogue, though, it can be amusing to use double negatives now and again; people often use them when they're talking. Listen out for examples of this or find examples in dialogue in your reading.

'Of' or 'have'?

We should **have** gone, since they could **have** taken us.

In the sentence above, notice the use of '**have**'.

When you say the sentence aloud, you will notice that the word 'have' gets swallowed up and sounds more like '**of**'. You must never write 'of' if you want to use correct grammar.

If you want to 'swallow' the 'have' to make it sound more like 'of', then use **contractions** in your writing. Using contractions, the example above would be written:

We should**'ve** gone, since they could**'ve** taken us.

How often do you write 'of' instead of 'have'? Look out for this error in your own writing!

> **REMEMBER!**
> Contractions are often used in dialogue.

Past tenses

These can cause problems because there are many **irregular** forms that do not follow familiar patterns. Listen to a three-year-old talking and you will hear some mistakes that crop up in older children's writing too!

"I hurted my knee and it bleeded so I did cry."

The three-year-old has not yet learned to say:

"I **hurt** my knee and it **bled** so I **cried**."

You need to learn irregular past tenses as you come across them. Here are some common irregular tenses that you should be familiar with:

Infinitive	Present tense	Past tense
to buy	I buy	I bought
to catch	you catch	you caught
to eat	he eats	he ate
to keep	she keeps	she kept

to make	it makes	it made
to run	we run	we ran
to speak	they speak	they spoke
to swim	they swim	they swam

Sometimes, when English is spoken, people will use different forms of the past tense. There is nothing wrong with these, but there are **standard forms** that you should know for 11+ English.

For instance, many people will say:

"I **done** my homework last night."

You need to know that in **Standard English** the correct way to say and write this is:

"I **did** my homework last night."

'I' or 'me'?

Many people find deciding on whether to use 'I' or '**me**' in a piece of writing challenging.

Look at these examples of children's writing:

Me and my brother went out to play football.

Su Lin and me handed in our homework on time.

When people are talking, they often make mistakes in these kinds of sentences. When you are writing, however, you need to show that you know whether to use 'I' or 'me'.

'I' must be used when you are the **subject** or one of the subjects of the sentence. (See page 55.) In the two sentences above, it would be clearly wrong to say, "Me went out to play football" or "Me handed in my homework on time", because you are the subject.

If you are doing something with someone else, then the other person's name comes first. That's only polite!

The correct versions of these two sentences should be:

My brother and I went out to play football.

Su Lin and I handed in our homework on time.

My aunt sent it to you and I.

Dad told Pete and I to wait for him.

'Me' must be used when you are the **object** of the sentence. If you split the sentences up into two, it makes it easier to see what is happening.

My aunt sent it to you. My aunt sent it to **me**.

Dad told Pete to wait for him. Dad told **me** to wait for him.

The correct versions of these two sentences should be:

My aunt sent it to **you and me**.

Dad told **Pete and me** to wait for him.

> **REMEMBER!**
>
> Always use 'me' after 'between': 'It is a secret between you and me.'

'Better' or 'best', 'worse' or 'worst', 'fewer' or 'less'?

These forms of adjectives can cause many people problems. You have to make sure that you use the correct form of the adjective when you are comparing.

These sentences are wrong: This jacket is the best of the two.

Sula is the worse chatterbox in the class.

Annie made less mistakes than Rob.

These sentences are correct: This jacket is **the better of** the two.

Sula is the **worst** chatterbox in the class.

Annie made **fewer** mistakes than Rob.

You are comparing two jackets, so that is why you need the **comparative** form 'better' rather than 'best'.

You need to use the **superlative** form, not the comparative form for describing Sula because there are more than two people in her class.

Use 'fewer' rather than 'less' to compare the number of mistakes made by Annie and Rob. You use 'less' for amounts of something but 'fewer' for numbers of things, e.g.

There's **less** water in your bottle than in Lucy's.

There are **fewer** bottles in the fridge today than there were yesterday.

(See page 52 for more details on how to form comparative adjectives.)

Look out for these adjective uses in your reading and try to use them correctly.

Spelling

In 11+ English you need to show that your spelling is as accurate as you can make it. It is important that you are careful and try to spell so that what you have to say can be understood by someone else.

The English language can be quite challenging to spell. Some people seem to be very good at it. They tend to be wide and attentive readers who are interested in words. Many people struggle. The words just won't stick.

> "I'm awful at spelling."

26 *Improving your spelling*

You will probably have had spellings to learn every week at school, so by Year 5 there will be many words that you can spell. No one is expecting you to be able to spell every word you write perfectly, but you do need to spell well enough to communicate in 11+ English.

✓ Be aware of the most common spelling errors.
(See page 66: *Learning awkward spellings*.)

✓ Learn the most important spelling rules, such as:
- **'i' before 'e' except after 'c' if it sounds like 'eee';**
- **When two vowels go a-walking, the first vowel does the talking.**

✓ Practise spellings using '**look say cover write check**'.

✓ Set yourself challenges: choose ten new useful words a week to learn using a spelling list.

✓ Sound out words in syllables; make up rhymes; march to them or clap them. (Spot syllables that are stressed and unstressed.)

✓ When learning a new word, ask yourself:
- Is it made up of familiar **smaller** words?
- Does it have a common letter string?
- Is it based on a common **root** word?
- Does it have a **prefix** or **suffix** you recognise?

✓ Group words in your mind and on paper, according to their letter patterns, e.g. **–ight, –ur, –ous, –tion**.

✓ Spot and learn silent letters in words like 'island', 'crumb', 'knock' or 'sword'.

✓ Try to make up **mnemonics** to help remember difficult words, for example '**b**irds **e**at **c**rumbs **a**s **u**ncle **s**its **e**ating' for 'because'.

✓ Get into the habit of using a dictionary, thesaurus or spellchecker to make sure that you have the right meaning and the right spelling.

✓ Practise spellings by enjoying wordsearches, crossword puzzles and word games.

> **REMEMBER!**
>
> Be interested in words and their spellings. Collect spellings of words you like and need to use.

27 *Learning awkward spellings*

These are some of the most awkward sets of spellings you need to be aware of for 11+ English:

- homophones
- doubling letters
- one letter misplaced
- frequent culprits

- magic 'e'
- singulars and plurals
- common letter strings
- homonyms

- adding prefixes
- adding suffixes
- '-shun' suffixes.
- silent letters, unstressed vowels

There is a section here on each of these with special hints and ideas for practice.

Look through all the sections that you are unsure about or need to brush up on.

Homophones

Homophones are words that sound exactly the same but are spelt differently and have different meanings. There are

> **REMEMBER!**
>
> 'Homo' means same; 'phone' means sound.

hundreds of homophones. They come in pairs and sometimes in groups of three or even four.

Here are some of the homophones that come up all the time and can cause confusion. People find them particularly tricky to spell because you have to be able to tell the difference between their meanings and spellings.

air/heir aloud/allowed are/our be/bee beech/beach board/bored
by/buy/bye caught/court course/coarse current/currant for/four flower/flour
great/grate hair/hare hole/whole its/it's key/quay
led/lead main/mane new/knew not/knot no/know our/hour
pale/pail past/passed practise/practice pray/prey principal/principle
rain/reign/rein right/write/rite road/rode/rowed route/root

saw/sore   seen/scene   serial/cereal   so/sew/sow   stationery/stationary
sun/son   their/there/they're   through/threw   thrown/throne   tide/tied
to/two/too   waist/waste   way/weigh   week/weak   where/wear
which/witch   whine/wine   who's/whose   would/wood   you/ewe/yew
you're/your

Pay special attention to learning homophones, both to their spellings and their meanings. It can help to:

> ✓ draw pictures next to the ones you find especially confusing
> ✓ make up reminders like: stationery has the letter 'e' for envelope in it.

Also look out for awkward homophones where one of the pair or group is spelled with an apostrophe. Be really careful about using these correctly.

Doubling letters

One of the most common spelling errors is forgetting to double a consonant when you need to keep the vowel sound short. Can you see which words have been spelled incorrectly in this sentence?

Jack was runing to put the rubish in the bin but at the beginning of the drive he sudenly spoted a funy chuby rabit sliping out of its burow.

Here are some hints that can help to remind you when to double consonants:

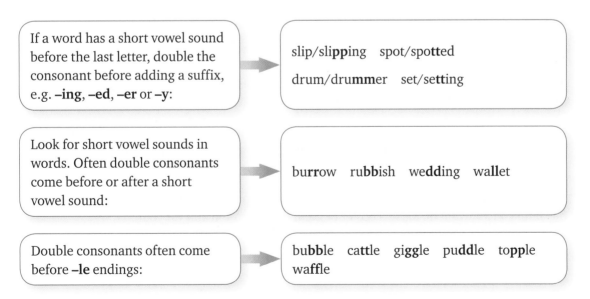

If a word has a short vowel sound before the last letter, double the consonant before adding a suffix, e.g. **–ing**, **–ed**, **–er** or **–y**:	slip/slip**p**ing spot/spot**t**ed drum/dru**mm**er set/se**tt**ing
Look for short vowel sounds in words. Often double consonants come before or after a short vowel sound:	bu**rr**ow ru**bb**ish we**dd**ing wa**ll**et
Double consonants often come before **–le** endings:	bu**bb**le ca**tt**le gi**gg**le pu**dd**le to**pp**le wa**ff**le

Here are some examples of words where both versions with or without the doubled consonant make sense. Look out for pairs of words like these and add to the list if you can.

shinning/shining	planned/planed	sitting/siting	hopping/hoping
pinning/pining	holly/holy	dinner/diner	latter/later
comma/coma	mopping/moping	tapped/taped	matting/mating
lopping/loping	starring/staring	ridding/riding	barring/baring
slopped/sloped	scarred/scared	dessert/desert	bidding/biding

One letter misplaced

It is amazing how often some word pairs are confused. Misplacing, leaving out or changing just one letter can alter the meaning of a sentence or make it difficult to understand. Read the word pairs below and really study the order of the letters.

Same letters, different order:

from/form	minuet/minute	quiet/quite
split/spilt	trial/trail	untie/unite

One letter more or less:

country/county	exciting/exiting	first/fist	learn/lean	of/off
started/stared	thorough/through	through/though	where/were	

One letter different:

pointed/painted	wander/wonder	where/there	effect/affect

Make sure that you check these kinds of words very thoroughly in your writing.

Frequent culprits

There may be words that always seem to let you down. Here are some examples of words that can be frequent culprits:

answer	beautiful	beginning	busy	definitely	describe	design
excellent	favourite	February	friend	necessary	separate	
special	tomorrow	usual				

If these (or other words) constantly let you down, try to practise them every day until you know them. Make a poster of them for your room and get your family to test you regularly.

Magic 'e' (split digraph)

Be aware of how the letter 'e' can completely change one word to make another by changing a short vowel sound into a long vowel sound.

Look at the examples below, which show how magic 'e' works. Say each pair aloud and listen to the difference the magic 'e' makes to the way you pronounce the words.

bar/bare	cloth/clothe	grim/grime	kit/kite	
pin/pine	quit/quite	rod/rode	scar/scare	
scrap/scrape	slid/slide	spit/spite	star/stare	strip/stripe

When the letter 'e' is at the end of a word, it doesn't always change the sound of the vowel. With many ancient words, such as '**come**', '**some**', '**gone**', and all the words ending in a '**v**' sound, such as '**have**', '**give**', '**love**', '**above**', '**twelve**', the final 'e' doesn't make a long vowel sound.

Notice the effect magic 'e' can also have on the letter '**g**' in these word pairs:

hug/ huge   rag/rage   stag/stage   wag/wage

It makes a long vowel sound but also makes the letter 'g' soft so that it sounds like '**j**'.

Here are some other words where magic 'e' affects the vowel and the letter 'g':

age   agent   courage   danger   digest   strange   stranger

Magic 'e' can have a similar effect on the letter '**c**', too. When a 'c' is followed by an 'e' it changes to a soft, hissing '**ss**' sound. Here are some words where magic 'e' affects the vowel and the letter 'c':

> **REMEMBER!**
>
> When letters 'c' or 'g' are followed by an 'i' or 'y', they can also make a soft sound.

ace	brace	disgrace	face	grace
lace	pace	place	race	replace
space	trace	dice	ice	lice
mice	nice	price	rice	slice
spice	twice	vice	puce	truce

Some words have both a hard and soft 'c' sound:

accident   access   concert   success

Singulars and plurals

You need to know how to make nouns plural. Many spelling errors at 11+ English are made by forming incorrect plurals. There are some simple rules you can learn.

> **REMEMBER!**
>
> Singular means **one**; plural means **more than one**.

| most plural nouns end in –s: | → | dogs   chairs   schools   computers |

| nouns ending in a hissing sound like –ch, –sh, –ss, –s or –x add –es: | → | church/churches   wish/wishes glass/glasses   bus/buses   box/boxes |

| nouns ending in a consonant + y change the –y to i and add –es: | → | baby/babies   berry/berries puppy/puppies |

| nouns ending in a vowel + y, add –s: | → | bay/bays   key/keys   valley/valleys |

| nouns ending in –a or –o add –s or –es: | → | camera/cameras   piano/pianos echo/echoes   tomato/tomatoes potato/potatoes   hero/heroes solo/solos |

| nouns ending in –f or –fe change the –f to a v and add –es: | → | shelf/shelves   scarf/scarves   life/lives |

REMEMBER!

There are some exceptions to this last rule which just add -s. These also need to be learned:
   chef/chefs
   belief/beliefs
   chief/chiefs
   handkerchief/handkerchiefs

REMEMBER!

Look out for words that have irregular plurals, e.g.:
   sheep/sheep   ox/oxen
   salmon/salmon   child/children
   woman/women   man/men
   tooth/teeth   foot/feet
   mouse/mice   trousers/trousers

Common letter strings

Many words share the same common letter strings but some spelling patterns can be a little harder to learn. Learning and recognising these patterns can help you to say and spell unfamiliar words.

Some of the more challenging spelling patterns are shown in the tables that follow.

Sounds like 'er'

er	ir	ur
her	bird	purse
certain	first	curl
term		

Here are two more letter strings that can make the same 'er' sound:
ear: early learn earth
wor: worth world worm worship

Sounds like 'or'

au	augh	aw	oar	oor	or	our
author	daughter	awful	soar	door	for	four
haul	taught	crawl	board	floor	story	court

Watch out for these exceptions: laugh, draught

Here are some more letter strings that can make the same 'or' sound:
ar: quarter
war: warm ('w' often changes the vowel sound in words)
See also the table for letter string '**ough**'.

atch/etch/itch/otch/utch

atch	etch	itch	otch	utch
batch	fetch	ditch	blotch	hutch
		kitchen		

Look out for exceptions such as:
atta**ch** ri**ch** sandwi**ch** whi**ch** mu**ch** su**ch** tou**ch**

ack/eck/ick/ock/uck

ack	eck	ick	ock	uck
lack	peck	pick	sock	luck
		sticker		

Notice exceptions such as:
brea**k**fast, te**ch**nique and words borrowed from other languages, e.g.:
tre**k** (Afrikaans)
wo**k** (Cantonese)

adge/edge/idge/odge/udge				
adge	edge	idge	odge	udge
badge	hedge	fridge	dodge	fudge

This next letter string can be especially tricky, as it is pronounced very differently in different words.

ough							
Sounds like: off	oh	oo	or	ow	uff	uh
	cough	dough	through	thought	bough	tough	borough

cious/tious/xious		
cious	tious	xious
suspicious	cautious	anxious
vicious		

Homonyms

These are words that are spelled exactly the same but have different meanings. Some are pronounced differently depending on their meanings.

Homonyms can cause confusion for readers. Sometimes you have to stress different syllables or change the vowel sounds to make the meanings clear. Look at these examples of homonyms.

Same pronunciation

bark/bark   block/block   club/club   fly/fly   form/form
jam/jam   leaves/leaves   train/train   watch/watch
waves/waves

> **REMEMBER!**
>
> These same **pronunciation** homonyms are often different parts of speech. (See page 49.)

Can you work out a different meaning for each word in these pairs? Here are some sentences that show the different meanings of three of these homonym pairs:

Sam watched the **fly fly** past the window.

He was making a **bark** rubbing when his dog began to **bark**.

I ate a **jam** sandwich while sitting in the traffic **jam**.

Different pronunciation

bow/bow	conduct/conduct	content/content	desert/desert
lead/lead	live/live	minute/minute	perfect/perfect
present/present	read/read	row/row	sow/sow
tear/tear	wind/wind	wound/wound	Polish/polish
entrance/entrance	invalid/invalid	denier/denier	

Do you know how each of these homonyms is pronounced? Here are some sentences that show the different meanings of three of these homonym pairs:

The guide will **lead** you to the **lead** mine.

In a **minute** you will hear a **minute** splash as the stone hits the bottom of the well.

The nurse **wound** a bandage around the boy's **wound**.

Silent letters and unstressed vowels

There are many words in English which have **silent letters** or unstressed vowels in them and you will need to pay particular attention to these, because simply sounding them out will not help you to spell them correctly.

On the next pages are some of the most common silent letters, with some handy hints that can help you think about where these letters can appear. Some useful silent letter words are given for each letter, but there are many more, so look out for them in your reading and writing.

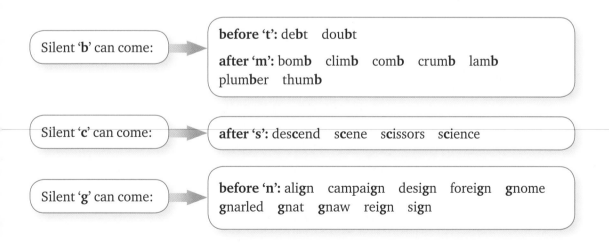

Silent 'b' can come:

before 't': de**b**t dou**b**t

after 'm': bom**b** clim**b** com**b** crum**b** lam**b** plum**b**er thum**b**

Silent 'c' can come:

after 's': des**c**end s**c**ene s**c**issors s**c**ience

Silent 'g' can come:

before 'n': ali**g**n campai**g**n desi**g**n forei**g**n **g**nome **g**narled **g**nat **g**naw rei**g**n si**g**n

Silent 'h' can come: →

after 'c': anchor   chaos   chemist   choir   psychology   school

after 'g': ghastly   ghost   ghoul   spaghetti   dinghy

after 'r': rhubarb   rhyme   rhythm   rhinoceros

after 'w': whale   wheat   when   which   while   whistle

Silent 'k' can come: →

before 'n': knead   knee   knife   knight   knit   knob   knock   know   knowledge   knot

Silent 'l' can come: →

before 'f': calf   half

before 'k': chalk   talk   walk   yolk

before 'm': balm   calm   palm

after 'ou': could   should   would

Silent 'n' can come: →

after 'm': autumn   hymn

Silent 's' can come: →

between 'i' and 'l': island   aisle

Silent 't' can come: →

before –le ending: castle   rustle   thistle   wrestle

before –en ending: christen   fasten   glisten   listen   moisten   soften

at the end of foreign words: ballet   chalet

Silent 'w' can come: →

before 'r': wrap   wreath   wreck   wren   wriggle   wrinkle   wrist   write   wrong   wrote

after 's': answer   sword

Making up mnemonics (short sentences, rhymes or silly stories) can help you remember the silent and unstressed letters in words. For instance:

Tom is at the back of the cas**t**le.
Noel stood at the back to sing the hym**n**.
The **wr**inkled **wr**en **wr**iggled on the **wr**ecked **wr**eath.

Try tracing over the **si**lent letters with a **si**lver pen to make them stick in your mind.

Unstressed vowels are not sounded clearly:

benefit (the second 'e' sounds like '**uh**')

Often they are not pronounced at all:

medicine (the first '**i**' is often '**swallowed**')

Read these examples of the two types aloud. Listen to what happens to the unstressed vowels. (They are highlighted in bold.)

'uh' vowels:

astron**o**my dand**e**lion gramm**a**r simil**a**r teleph**o**ne

'swallowed' vowels:

jewell**e**ry fact**o**ry short**e**ning int**e**rest mini**a**ture fam**i**ly

Adding prefixes

You need to know the meanings of some of the most common prefixes as they may help you to understand the meanings of some unfamiliar words. Not all prefixes have particular meanings but you should know the most common ones:

Prefix	Examples		
auto– means self	automatic	autograph	autobiography
bi– or **di–** mean two or twice	bicycle	dissect	bilingual
circ–/circum– means about or round	circle	circus	circumstance
co–/con– means with or together	cooperate	congregate	conversion

pre– means before	predict prefix preface
re– means again	repeat rebuild replace
sub– means under	submarine submit submerge
tele– means far off or distant	telephone television telescope
trans– means across	transatlantic transform transport

These prefixes are all used to make **antonyms** (opposites). (See page 58.)

anti– means against	anticlockwise antidote antiseptic
de– means making the opposite of	decode deform demist
dis– means not or making the opposite of	disappear dislike distrust
mis– means wrong or false	misbehave misplace mistake
non– means not or opposite of	non-fiction nonsense non-stick
un– means not	unable unfit unlikely

Adding suffixes

You need to know the most common suffixes:

–able   –ed   –er   –est   –ful   –ing

–less   –ly   –ment   –tion

> **REMEMBER!**
>
> A suffix is a group of letters added to the end of a word to change its meaning.

Some of these can be added without changing the spelling of the root word (e.g. **–ful**, **–less**, **–ment**) but sometimes changes to the root word are needed. Here are some general rules which can help you to work out what these changes are and when they are needed. Remember: most rules have exceptions!

REMEMBER!

Remember the rule for adding suffixes to words that end in 'e': Ends in 'e', delete the 'e'!

For suffixes beginning with an '**a**', '**e**' or '**i**':

If the root ends with an 'e', drop the 'e' then add the suffix.

love → lov**able**   lov**ed**   lov**er**   lov**ing**

If the root ends with a short vowel sound followed by a single consonant, double the consonant then add the suffix (see *Doubling letters*, page 78):

shop → sho**pped**   sho**pper**   sho**pping**

For suffixes **–er**, **–est**, **–ly** or **–ness**:

If the root ends with a '**y**', change the '**y**' to '**i**' then add the suffix.

happy → happ**ier**   happ**iest**   happ**ily**   happ**iness**

For the suffix **–tion**:

If the root ends with an '**e**', drop the '**e**' then add the suffix:

introduce → introdu**ction**

If the root ends with '**t**' or '**te**', drop these letters then add the suffix:

educate → educa**tion**

Some root endings will need to be changed further:

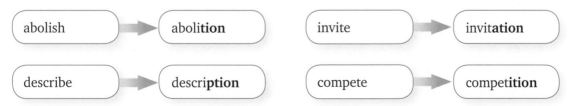
abolish → aboli**tion**   invite → invit**ation**

describe → descri**ption**   compete → compet**ition**

Some root words can take several different suffixes. Each suffix changes the meaning of the word.

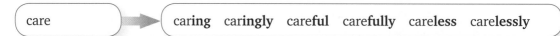

care → caring caringly careful carefully careless carelessly

Sometimes the 'e' at the end of a root word needs to be kept before adding a suffix or else the meaning is changed. Notice what happens to these words if you drop the 'e':

dye → dyeing → singe → singeing

'–shun' suffixes

Several different suffixes make the same 'shun' sound but they are all spelled differently.

Words ending in these letter strings can be rather tricky to spell:

–tion –ssion –cian –sion (this one often sounds a bit different from the others!)

Here are some rules to help you work out which is the right ending to use:

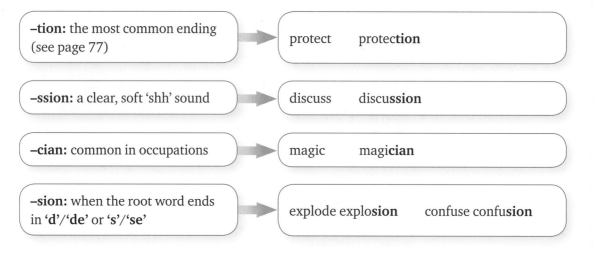

–tion: the most common ending (see page 77) → protect protec**tion**

–ssion: a clear, soft 'shh' sound → discuss discu**ssion**

–cian: common in occupations → magic magi**cian**

–sion: when the root word ends in **'d'/'de'** or **'s'/'se'** → explode explo**sion** confuse confu**sion**

Exam tips

Instead of using the same words all of the time, it is good to develop your vocabulary by learning words that are new to you and knowing how to use them in a sentence. You could replace 'very big' with 'huge' or 'expansive'. You could replace 'really bad' with 'terrible' or 'horrendous'. In an exam, don't worry too much about a word you know but are unsure of spelling. It is better to write the word 'miniture' for 'miniature' than to just write 'tiny' as it shows you know the word and how to use it properly.

Cloze tests

In 11+ English you may come across Cloze tests. They are especially common in CEM exams. Cloze tests are where a text has a missing word or phrase. Either you are given the words or phrases to add in the correct places, or you may have to think of a suitable word or phrase yourself. To solve cloze test exercises you will need wide-ranging vocabulary skills, grammar skills and the ability to select the right word for the right place.

(28) *Words given in a box*

Look at this example:

> Add the following words to the correct places in the text so that the extract makes sense. Each word must be used only once.
>
> | between | boarded | corridor | dismay |
> |---------|---------|----------|--------|
> | reserved | squashed | still | |
>
> As we _____ the train to London, we noted with _____ the number of people who were _____ into every seat, every aisle and in every _____. We moved _____ carriages and _____ we could not find a seat. I could have kicked myself for not having _____ a seat, especially when it was during the holiday season.

One strategy for solving this type of question is to read the list of words and then to read the extract to get a clear idea of the topic. Reread the extract placing the correct word in the correct place. Finally, read though the text one last time to make sure the extract makes sense.

<table>
<tr><td>REMEMBER!</td><td>REMEMBER!</td></tr>
<tr><td>Look for spelling clues. For example, if you have an answer line following the word 'an' you know the word you are looking for begins with a vowel or a silent 'h'.</td><td>Look for word class clues. For example, if you have a list and the word 'and', you may need to look for a word similar in class to the others in the list, e.g. a noun, an adjective, or a verb. If you have an article like 'a' or 'the' in front of a missing word, you are probably looking for a noun or an adjective; if you have a verb that is being described, you are looking for an adverb.</td></tr>
</table>

29 *Underlining phrases*

Look at this example:

> Underline the correct phrases that fit into the spaces in the text so that the extract makes sense.
>
> Looking around at the dreadful mess, I [A] cried! I had never [B] so awful! Sticky blobs of syrup [C] the kitchen top and on to the floor.
>
> **A**
>
> [can of]   [can have]   [could of]   [could have]
>
> **B**
>
> [saw anything]   [seen anything]   [seed anything]   [see anything]
>
> **C**
>
> [drips off]   [drips of]   [dripped off]   [dripped of]

These questions really require you to know your grammar well. Do double check that you have the correct tense and always read the extract back to yourself to ensure it makes sense.

30 *Finding your own word*

Look at this example:

> Find one word that fits into each space so that the extract makes sense.
>
> The _____ loved looking after the animals. His father and his grandfather before him had owned the same breeds of cattle and sheep as he did now and he hoped one day that at least one of his own _____ would take on the business. Waking up before dawn and watching the _____ rise still thrilled him and at the end of the day when the sky was streaked with orange, pink and red, he felt pleasure at the thought of the following beautiful day. It was true that he worked extremely long _____, but this job was in his blood.

Although coming up with your own answers may feel impossible, the extract will be full of clues to help you. The best strategy is to read the extract to find out what it is about and to then think of what words could possibly fit into the spaces. Most of the time there will only be one possible answer that makes sense, and at other times there could be a couple of possibilities. If more than one answer would make sense, then whichever option you choose will gain marks. Start by looking for clues:

The _____ loved looking after the animals.

Who looks after animals? A zookeeper, dog walker, farmer, shepherd, pet shop owner?

Are there any other clues about the animals? Yes: cattle and sheep are mentioned, so this isn't a zookeeper or a dog walker. There are cattle as well as sheep, so this isn't a shepherd. It isn't a pet shop owner, so this must be 'farmer'.

…he hoped one day that at least one of his own _____ would take on the business.

The words 'father' and 'grandfather' appear, so the text is talking about the farm being passed down through the generations. The missing word must be another family member who is younger than the father. The phrase 'at least one' shows this word must be plural. The words 'children', 'sons' or 'daughters' would work here.

Waking up before dawn and watching the _____ rise…

The clues are a period of time 'before dawn' and being able to watch something 'rise'. This sentence talks about the very early morning when the sun rises; so the missing word must be 'sun'.

It was true that he worked extremely long _____, but this job was in his blood.

The text so far has been about the farmer getting up before the sun and then watching the sunset. That gives you a clue about his working life. What would fit with 'he worked extremely long…'? The words that fit would either be 'days' or 'hours' – some unit of time that makes sense in the extract.

Although this type of cloze test where you come up with words to fill the gaps looks a little scary, there are plenty of clues to help you find a suitable word. Make sure that you look for each clue and then check your extract at the end. Here is one example of this completed extract:

The **farmer** loved looking after the animals. His father and his grandfather before him had owned the same breeds of cattle and sheep as he did now and he hoped one day that at least one of his own **children** would take on the business. Waking up before dawn and watching the **sun** rise still thrilled him and at the end of the day when the sky was streaked with orange, pink and red, he felt pleasure at the thought of the following beautiful day. It was true that he worked extremely long **hours,** but this job was in his blood.

Everyday practice: English

There are many activities that you can do to help your child with the 11+ exam. Building their knowledge through experiences and opportunities is far better than sitting and learning lists. Some of these activities underpin 11+ knowledge and concepts while other activities help to provide a more holistic education.

Reading fun

Introduce your child to a wide range of literature, e.g. stories, poems, non-fiction, comics, etc. This will deepen their understanding of the world and build their vocabulary skills. Encourage your child to talk to you about what they are reading and why they like, or dislike, it.

Find a funny story or passage to read to or with your child and discuss the meaning, bearing in mind the **five Ws**: **who** the characters are; **where** and **when** the passage is taking place; **what** is happening; **why** the characters are acting as they do (their feelings and motivation).

Games and activities

Board or pieces games

These games use either a board or games pieces/tiles. They extend skills in spelling, vocabulary, and knowledge of word definitions in the most fun way. Examples include: Scattergories, Bananagrams, Articulate, Countdown, Boggle, Dabble, Brainbox English, Scrabble (both Junior Scrabble and the standard version are popular).

Console, computer, phone games

These portable games are played by one child and can extend and consolidate English skills. There are many games and apps that cover spelling, word knowledge, anagrams, etc., but games such as Big Brain Academy and Buzz Brain are popular.

Pencil and paper games

These are quicker games to play and are portable. You just need a pencil and some paper. You can vary the games according to the age and ability of your child. Some examples of paper games that extend English skills include: Consequences, Telephone Pictionary, Riddles, Target ("How many words of three letters or more can you make from the word 'DICTIONARY'?"), Categories ("Can you name five or ten items that fit into categories such as 'ball games', 'authors', 'buildings'?" Then make the game more challenging by choosing categories such as 'citrus fruit' or 'root vegetables').

Car games

Although many children might play paper games or online games when they are travelling, you can also use games like these:

- **Car registration names** – trying to find the funniest descriptive name using the last three letters of the car registration plate, e.g. ABC could be Adorably Beautiful Clara or Awfully Boring Cain; both work as they have one or two descriptive words plus a name. You can vary this game to include place names, sports or food, for example.
- **Place names** – "Who can create the best story of how a place got its name in two minutes?" The most creative, or funniest, wins.
- **I'm going on a journey** – this involves adding one item at a time to create a memory list of items, which is a great way to develop descriptive vocabulary. The first person says, "I'm going on a journey and will take…" They add an item, then the second person repeats this and adds their own item, to the end. You might end up with the sixth person saying, "I'm going on a journey and will take: a multicoloured beach ball, a blue bucket and spade, a tartan picnic blanket, a giant inflatable shark, a big bag of barley sugar AND a little bottle of hand gel." The more creative the better!

Days in

- Help your child to be a news reporter for the day: let them think of questions to interview you, then write up the interview.
- Go on a virtual holiday: encourage your child to imagine an island, draw it and describe the trips out and activities holidaymakers can do. Ask them to imagine the hotels or campsites available. Your child can create a currency, a language, menus for restaurants and write a postcard to send home as if they had spent a fortnight at the resort.
- Allow your child access to the Internet with supervision for an hour to find as many facts as they can about any topic you choose, e.g. a place; a famous person; a famous event; an animal, bird, fish or insect; a building or a period of time.

Other hands-on activities

Further examples of hands-on activities that a child can do by him- or herself and that help to strengthen key English skills include:

- word searches and crosswords
- puzzle books (the Bond Brain Training Word Puzzle book is perfect for developing English skills)
- scrapbooking (collating recipes, slogans, diary entries, poetry or stories)
- keeping diaries, corresponding with penfriends, or entering writing competitions.

Top ten everyday activities

1 Discuss with your child how he or she reacts emotionally in different situations. This can be quite revealing and a starting place to describe emotions that can be used for storytelling.

2 When watching television shows, listen for differences between formal and informal speech.

3 Ask your child to look at all the compound words they use during the day and to draw attention to them. Whether it is going 'upstairs' to their 'bedroom' or 'outside' to build a 'snowman' or to play 'football' they might actively try looking for compound words.

4 When watching television or a film, ask your child to notice what characters say and how they say it. It can make writing realistic dialogue easier.

5 If you are selling an item online, ask your child to help you write an effective description that would appeal to a potential buyer.

6 If you are passing by an estate agent's window, look at the description used and contract it as much as possible, removing all the descriptive words, e.g. 'With a delightful, lovely low-maintenance garden,' becomes 'Has a small garden.'

7 Read a newspaper or news website with your child and then discuss it together. 'First News' is an ideal introduction and many school libraries stock it. Questions that are not open-ended are best, e.g.: "What effect do you think this new housing estate will have?"

8 Ask your child to give a title to a meal, then describe the meal with rich, evocative language that appeals to the senses.

9 Encourage your child to ask questions about your job, your family, running a home or how your day has been, and answer them with enough detail, at an understandable level, so that they expand their knowledge and vocabulary and hear examples of descriptive words.

10 Try watching a cartoon or pre-school-age programme with the volume turned off and see how much of the programme your child understands from non-verbal communication. Ask them how they have worked out their response and what actions or expressions were most useful.

Glossary

abbreviation – a shortened version of a word or phrase.

abstract noun – a concept or idea; something that cannot be seen, heard or touched.

acronym – the first letters of words put together as a short version and said as a single word.

active – where someone or something is actually doing something.

adjectival phrase – a group of words with the adjective as head of the phrase, e.g. He looked at the *huge, fluffy, grey* cat.

adjective – a word used to describe a noun.

adverb – a word usually used to describe a verb.

adverbial phrase – a group of words with the adverb as head of the phrase, e.g. The car rolled down the hill *gently at first and then quicker and quicker* as it built momentum.

alliteration – the use of the same letter or sound at the beginning of words that are close together.

antonym – a word with an opposite meaning to another word.

auxiliary verbs – parts of the verbs 'to be' or 'to have' which go with other verbs to help make a tense.

character – a person in a story, play script or other kind of narrative text.

chronologically – in order of time, from first event to last

clause – a simple sentence that has a subject and an active verb. It can stand alone or be part of a longer sentence.

cliffhanger – an ending to a story or piece of writing which leaves the reader guessing about what may happen next.

collective noun – a word that stands for a group or collection of things.

common noun – a word that is a general name for a person, place, feeling, thing or event.

comparative adjective – a word that is used to compare two things.

complex – more complicated.

compound word – two or more words put together to make a new idea.

conjunction – a word used to join together two or more clauses in a sentence.

connective – a word or phrase used to join together two or more clauses in a sentence.

contraction – when two or more words are joined together to make just one word, using apostrophes to show any missing letters, e.g. do not = don't.

determiner – an article (a, an, the), a demonstrative (this, those, that), a number (one, ten, thirty-six), an ordinal (first, next, last), a possessive (his, our, my, your) or a quantifier (all, none, some, every) that we place before a noun.

dialogue – a conversation between two or more characters in a story.

dilemma – a problem which needs to be solved.

diminutive – a small or young version of something or somebody.

direct speech – the actual words people say to each other.

double negative – saying no twice, so that it means yes.

exception – something which does not follow common rules.

expanded phrase – a phrase that has additional information.

feedback – advice and comments given by someone else in response to a piece of writing.

feminine – female, like a girl or a woman.

first person – using 'I' or 'we'.

formal – following rules; polite.

fronted adverbial – a word, or short phrase, that can be placed at the beginning of a sentence for effect, e.g. It was raining earlier. = Earlier, it was raining.

gender – tells whether something is male or female.

head word – the main or most important word in a phrase

homonym – a word that sounds the same as another and is spelled the same but has a different meaning.

homophone – a word that sounds the same as another but has a different meaning and is spelled differently.

imagery – words used to bring pictures into the reader's mind.

imperative – the 'command' form of a verb e.g. 'Run!'

indefinite pronoun – a word that stands for a noun but not a particular one, e.g. everything/something/anything, etc.

indent – show the start of a paragraph by beginning the first line of writing a little further to the right of the margin than the other lines.

infer – work out meaning from the clues in a text, even though the exact meaning is not given.

infinitive – the basic form of a verb starting with 'to', e.g. to give, to think.

informal – relaxed and chatty.

introduction – the beginning of a piece of writing, setting the scene or introducing characters or ideas.

inverted commas – (also known as speech marks or quotation marks) the marks (" " or ' ') we add before and after words spoken.

irregular – not following the usual rules.

Latin – an old language spoken by the Romans over two thousand years ago which forms the root of many of our English words.

layout – the visual organisation of text according to the text type, such as poem, play, diary entry, report, etc.

legibly – able to be read easily.

letter string – letters that commonly go together to make certain sounds.

main clause – part of a sentence which contains a verb.

margin – a blank border at the left-hand side of a page.

masculine – male, like a boy or a man.

metaphor – a word or phrase used to describe something as if it was something else.

mnemonic – a way of remembering things which are difficult to remember.

modal verbs – words such as *could, would, should, shall* and *might* that help modify other verbs.

moral – a lesson that stories like fables teach a reader.

narrator – the person telling the story.

negative – not good or positive; the reverse of something; saying no or not.

noun – a naming word.

noun phrase – a group of words with the noun as head of the phrase, e.g. *Tired and irritated, the head of Year 6* shut the cupboard door with a bang.

object – who or what is being affected by the subject and the verb in a sentence.

onomatopoeic – sounding the same as its meaning.

paragraph – a sentence or set of sentences describing one stage of a piece of writing, separated from the next paragraph either by a line space or an indent.

parenthesis – adding extra information to a sentence, between a pair of dashes or a pair of brackets.

passive – where someone or something is having something done to them.

personal pronoun – a word that stands for a noun and shows who, e.g. I/me, we/us, they/them, etc.

persuasive writing – a piece of writing which tries to make the reader share a point of view.

phrase – a group of words which has a meaning but is not a complete sentence.

plot – the problem or dilemma developed in a story.

plural – more than one.

positive – good; saying yes or definitely.

possessive pronoun – a word that stands for a noun and shows to whom it belongs, e.g. mine, yours, his, hers, etc.

predict – decide what may happen next, using clues in the text to support what you say.

prefix – a group of letters added in front of a root word to change its meaning.

preposition – a word that shows the position, direction or timing of a noun.

pronoun – a word used instead of a noun: he, it, they, we, you, she, I, etc.

pronunciation – how you say a word.

proper noun – a special name (or title) of a person, place or thing.

prose – a piece of continuous writing.

recount – a retelling of a series of events.

relative clause – a clause that uses a relative pronoun such as who, when, that, which to join additional information to a noun phrase, e.g. She saw the cat, *which was in its basket.*

relative pronoun – a word that stands for a noun and introduces a clause telling more about it.

reported (indirect) speech – what people say to each other, but not in the actual words they use.

root word – the main part of a word to which prefixes and/or suffixes can be added.

sentence – a group of words that go together to make sense, usually starting with a capital letter and ending with a full stop.

silent letter – a letter that cannot be heard in a spoken word.

simile – a phrase used to compare one thing with another using 'like' or 'as … as'.

singular – only one.

Standard English – a form of English which is used as a world language and a guide for correct usage, especially in writing and formal speech.

stanza - a group of lines in a poem

strategy – a way of working out a problem.

structure – the shape of a piece of writing and how it is organised.

subject – who or what is doing the action of the verb in a sentence.

subjunctive form – a tense which uses 'were' instead of 'was' to express hopes, dreams or wishes, e.g. *If I were the Prime Minister, I would make new laws.*

subordinate clause – part of a sentence that adds meaning to the main clause but cannot be used as a sentence on its own.

suffix – a group of letters added after a root word to change its meaning.

superlative adjective – a word that is used to describe the most, the biggest, the best, the worst, etc.

syllable – part of a word that contains at least one vowel and makes one sound.

synonym – a word with a similar meaning to another word.

technique – a way of doing things.

tense – used to show if a verb is in the past, present or future.

third person – using 'he', 'she' or 'they'.

time adverbials – adverbs such as *first, next, later, tomorrow* that help to structure time and order.

topic – something to write, learn or talk about.

unstressed vowel – a vowel that is not clear when a word is spoken.

verb – an action word that shows doing, having or being.

vocabulary – words; the range of words that a person knows and can use.

OXFORD
UNIVERSITY PRESS

Great Clarendon Street, Oxford, OX2 6DP, United Kingdom

Oxford University Press is a department of the University of Oxford.
It furthers the University's objective of excellence in research, scholarship,
and education by publishing worldwide. Oxford is a registered trade mark
of Oxford University Press in the UK and in certain other countries

British Library Cataloguing in Publication Data
Data available

ISBN: 978-0-19-277614-3

10 9 8 7 6 5 4 3 2

Paper used in the production of this book is a natural, recyclable product
made from wood grown in sustainable forests. The manufacturing process
conforms to the environmental regulations of the country of origin.

Printed in China

Acknowledgements

The Publishers would like to thank Michellejoy Hughes for her contribution to this edition.

Cover illustrations by Lo Cole